PSYCHOLOGY OF LANGUAGE
A Local Habitation and a Name

BY THE SAME AUTHOR

The Foundations of Human Nature (Longmans, Green and Co., 1935).

Living Consciously, with Walter H. Seegers (Detroit: Wayne State University Press, 1959).

The Growth of Self Insight (Detroit: Wayne State University Press, 1960).

The Jefferson-Dunglison Letters (Charlottesville, Va.: University of Virginia Press, 1960).

Illness of Allness (Detroit: Wayne State University Press, 1965).

American Government, Conscious Self Sovereignty (Detroit: Center for Health Education, 1969).

Psychology of Emotion (Detroit: Center for Health Education, 1971).

Monographs

Science of Sanity (Detroit: Center for Health Education, 1954).

Living Education (Detroit: Center for Health Education, 1957).

Discovering My World of My Mind, A Conscious Way of Life (Detroit: Center for Health Education, 1965).

PSYCHOLOGY OF LANGUAGE

A Local Habitation and a Name

John M. Dorsey, M.D., LL.D.

**Published by
Center for Health Education
4421 Woodward Avenue
Detroit, Michigan 48201**

Printed by Edwards Brothers, Inc.

iii

Cover symbol designed by Richard Kinney

Now for my life, it is a miracle of thirty years, which to relate were not a history, but a piece of poetry, and would sound to common ears like a fable. . . . The world that I regard is myself; it is the microcosm of my own frame that I cast mine eye on; for the other, I use it but like my globe, and turn it round sometimes, for my recreation . . . there is purely a piece of divinity in us. . . . Nature tells me, I am the image of God, as well as Scripture. He that understands not thus much hath not his introduction or first lesson, and is yet to begin the alphabet of man.

Sir Thomas Browne, Religio Medici

CONTENTS

PREFACE

Why all this preface?

Euripides, *Iphigenia among the Tauri*

Why indeed, except I am sure my story of my language also requires it. In this literary adventure I bravely record my study of certain elements I use in my language, wishing fact after fact to speak for its own originality and sufficiency. I regard nothing as acquired, everything as natural, consciousness for the naturalness of anything often being hard to come by. Homer sang it all in one verse. "I have learnt from none but myself" (*Odyssey*, 22, 347).

This present literary growth of mine naturally follows *Psychology of Emotion*[1] in which I was constantly challenging my way of wording my self feeling, finally deciding any or all of my behavior to be not only emotional but *emotion itself.* I note the extent to which Aristotle's *Rhetoric* concerns itself with emotion. I also note Aristotle's distinction in his *Rhetoric* (Bk. 1, Ch. 2, 1333–35), "the theory of rhetoric is concerned not with what seems probable to a given life like Socrates or Hippia, but with what seems probable to men of a given type." However, Aristotle's conception of rhetoric is: eloquent public speaking, "rhetor" meaning orator. For him rhetorical study concerns modes of persuasion: "Rhetoric may be defined as the faculty of observing in any given case the available means of persuasion. This is not a function of any other art."

My discovery of the nature and grounds of my language is the consequence of my awakening to my truth that all I can ever experience in any way whatever, comes under the one and only heading of my growing my self. All that I can do is be, and all I can be is what I grow of me. My language can be only a sign, conscious or unconscious, of my necessary self sufficiency, quite as is all that precedes my growing to verbalize my

---

[1] John M. Dorsey, Detroit: Center for Health Education, 1971.

ix

sensing, perceiving, feeling, thinking, doing, wishing. The intensity of my feeling of belief, of the rightness of my conviction, about any of my experience, is the measure of my identifying it with my *conscious* individuality. I readily consider "believe" and "belove" to be congeners. My enjoyment in my *conscious self* fulfillment, once discovered, can be cultivated by my practicing it. My John Ciardi sensed, "A man is finally defined by what he does with his attention."

No one of my world can prove the existence of anything except his own self experience. At most he can claim that belief in his solipsistic individuality is inconceivable, knowing that inconceivability proves nothing. However, he can always identify his personal conviction with objective validity, since his language seems undeniably objectified merely by making his mind conform with the grammar of his language.

In his charmingly enlightening Preface to his nobly great innovation, *A Dictionary of the English Language,* Samuel Johnson provides an excellent account of the nature of words derived from *the wells of English undefiled,* "sounds are too volatile and subtile for legal restraints, and to lash the wind, are equally the undertakings of pride, unwilling to measure its desires by its strength . . . no dictionary of a living tongue ever can be perfect, since while it is hastening to publication, some words are budding, and some falling away."

The Preface to the fourth edition of *The American Language* by H. L. Mencken (New York: Alfred A. Knopf, 1937, p. vi) contains notable discussion of the powerful philologian's observation of the changing growth of his language, English and American. When he was first interested in the subject (1910), "the American form of the English language was plainly departing from the parent stem" and seemed likely to continue. "This was what I argued in my first three editions. But since 1923 the pull of American has become so powerful that it has begun to drag English with it, and in consequence, some of the differences once visible have tended to disappear." The Englishman, "of late, has yielded so much to American example, in vocabulary, in idiom, in spelling and even in pronunciation," that his language "promises to become . . . a kind of dialect of American . . . ."

Entirely too occasional is published protest against my use of language to conceal my personal identity, along with its evident personal responsibility. As semanticist I have not yet learned how to compete with the noise of my mass-media nor am I even sufficiently convinced of the really awful consequence of the extent of my unconscious use of my vocabulary (or rather, my depersonalized vocabulary's use of my will). Nevertheless my fellowman is issuing many a warning about how extremely dangerous it is for anyone to neglect disciplining his mind with conscious appreciation for the personal nature of his every word. However, in all conscious self education, quite as William Hamilton affirmed, "the comparative utility of a study is not to be *principally* estimated by the complement of truths which it may communicate; but by the degree in which it determines our higher capacities to action."[2]

In his strongly worded essay, "The Limitations of Language,"[3] Melvin Maddocks describes a new disease entity he calls "semantic aphasia" in which words seem "to cause more misunderstandings than they prevent," producing

> the monstrous insensitivity that allows generals to call war "pacification," union leaders to describe strikes or slowdowns as "job actions," and politicians to applaud even moderately progressive programs as "revolutions" . . . . With proud humility today's dictionary editor abdicates even as arbiter, refusing to recognize any standards but usage. If enough people misuse disinterested as a synonym for uninterested, Webster's will honor it as a synonym . . . .Mankind craves definition as he craves lost innocence. He simply does not know what his life means until he says it. Until the day he dies he will grapple with mystery by trying to find the word for it.

[2] *Discussions on Philosophy and Literature.* New York: Harper and Bros., 1868, p. 47.
[3] *Time,* March 8, 1971, pp. 36, 37.

Herbert J. Muller writes revealingly,[4]

> The state of language reflects all the basic disorders in our world, the chaos underlying the most elaborate forms or appearances of order . . . . In general, popular language at its worst is suited to a technological age chiefly as an illustration of the stereotyped complaints about a standardized, mechanized society, all the "massmen" whose sensibilities have been dulled and who have no style of their own because no personal identity . . . . The habitual use of the impersonal and the passive voice ("It is advised that") is a way of blurring or evading responsibility . . . .

Professor Muller aptly quotes Jacques Barzun's humorous barb at his educationists, that fifty years ago they borrowed the term focus from photography "and we have not had a clear statement from them since."

I am not born with appreciation for the soul, or whole, of me, and I deem it the specific purpose of my living to *create* for my self this realization. My language serves me well for my cultivating my rightful self discovery, self recognition, provided that I discipline my mind to make it (my language) consciously subject to me and of me. Investing my love in words in which I cannot find my self, e.g., the impersonal language of technology, obstructs my appreciation for my life itself. William Heard Kilpatrick states this feeling heartily,[5] "To make the best individuality possible—this is at least one way of stating the whole duty of man."

Ever since first devoting my attention to my way of wording my mind I have startled my self with my boldness in exposing insincerity that I have been indulging as sincerity. My word "memory" provides a difficultly felt illustration. As long as I could continue using this term only as if it refers to my "past" living I troubled my self very little with it. However my mental modification called "consciousness" enlightens my mind so that it can be seen for what it *is,* quickens my mind so that it

---

[4] "The State of Language," *Virginia Quarterly Review,* 45, No. 3 (Summer, 1969), 386–401.
[5] *Selfhood and Civilization.* New York: Macmillan Co., 1941, p. 203.

can be felt for what it *is,* and frees my mind so that it can act for what it *is.* My living my term "memory" with my "consciousness" reveals it as entirely and only my *present* living. That means that it can be of no significance whatsoever for my so called past living, despite all of my illusion that it concerns only and entirely my past living. My new orientation for my word "memory" entails my taking very considerable trouble to understand what I am *presently* living when I seem to be only remembering.

"Past" cannot exist, only *present* can exist. All of "history" can have meaning only for present living. What is past, is prologue—can be true only in the sense of its *present* being. There is but one tense possible, my *present* tense. So-called past or future tense derives all of its significance from its being lived now and here. Of such good fortune is the providence of present living.

This sincere meaning of memory holds me accountable *now* for whatever I "recall." My illusional concept of memory becomes understandable as my defense against my uniting as my present self identity whatever I prefer to dislocate in my so-called past life. It also explains why, chameleon-like, my so-called memory for events, names, etc., varies with my living of each fellowman. This true assessment of my meaning for memory is most valuable for my understanding my wonderful process termed "free association."[6]

My need for a conception of my self arises from my recognizing certain continuity of love in my living of my subjectivity, despite the variety of its modifications. This recognition is possible through apperception, my present living seeming to be able to revive my past, as in my illusion of memory. My denial that the total significance of memory is its significance for my *present* living is tantamount to repressing the emotion of the self experience involved.

It now begins to become evident that what I mean by "psychology of language" is actually an expression of my profound

[6] Lifesaving discovery by Sigmund Freud providing scientific method for making unconscious mind conscious: self analysis.

interest in initiating some of my conscious psychology for some of my conscious language. This approach to developing individual life appreciation, my everyone's most dangerous desideratum, opens up for me fresh self vistas in every direction of my mind. My power of attention to make my own mind the *conscious subject of its own operations* starts an entirely new set of demands upon my language to make itself a definite vocabulary for naming my own conscious self living. I *am* always only minding my own business, but I need consciousness for that abiding truth.

My consciousness is my mind's awareness for its own modification. My full or complete consciousness recognizes my mind's awareness for its modifications *as such.* In distinguishing self from not-self I can only distinguish some of my mind from something else of my mind. My mind cannot operate beyond the sphere of itself. By dividing my mind into 1) what I can name mind, and 2) what I cannot name mind, I necessitate conceiving a reality other than mental that I nominate as some substantial material other than mental. Thus arises my need for my illusion of external reality, instead of my consciously imagined external reality.

It is of very greatest importance for everyone that *anyone* be able to experience his own personal life in a way that clearly convinces him of its priceless worth.

Seemingly wanton risking or destroying of human life, prenatal or post natal, can become understandable only in terms of the destroyer's low estimate of the worth of *his* personal living. I find that my liking or disliking this view is entirely beside the point, having absolutely nothing to do with it. My feeling of liking can refer only to its self, although it is specifically life affirming in nature; my feeling of disliking, which is only my inhibited liking, can refer only to its self, and it is specifically life inhibiting in nature.[7]

The significance of this emotional orientation is stupendous, and therefore it is only seldom realized. My illegal and legalized crime are the resulting symptoms warning me of the stu-

[7] *Psychology of Emotion,* p.xxiv.

pendous cost of stupendous self disesteem. Apart from its desirable meaning as a helpful symptom my overworked word "crime," as every other pejorative or meliorative, is a void name bare of possibility other than that of denominating my sparing my feeling my self responsibility.

Raising all of my emotional living, in a philological sense, to my recognizable *self* category contributes directly to my fullest development of its biological adequacy. Pending my nominally supported revelation of my solipsistic greatness the highest self esteem I can name hints at self sacrifice. Thus I let duty make shift for the pleasure of being certain that I am *always* behaving exactly as I please, that all of my experience is the creative exposition of my every wish.

Whoever verbally embodies in the total sum of all of his living the greatest sense of his personal identity, naturally glories in his awareness for his imagining his own divinity. By continuing to name my own living consciously mine, I find that I achieve all possible in making my republic of letters serve my sanity as American, including World, citizen.

My uncritical acceptance of innumerable words denoting not-self is of far greater than mere verbal interest. Rather my every word enters into my nomenclature for my science of my mind itself. All of my science is nothing but my (mental) theorizing, my practicing my innovation of knowledge upon my self. Rather than regarding my mind as a means for advancing my learning, I consider all of my so-called study to be merely my discipline furthering my mental development. Although all of my mind that must depend upon language can be only that language itself, it is all the more indicated that I do not allow my vocabulary to appear to be able to take over any, much less all, of my mental power. As George Dalgarno felt (*Ars Signorum,* 1661), "the soul can exert her powers by the ministry of any of the senses."

It is only by living self consciously that I can develop any feeling of conviction in what I mean by *personal.* Furthermore it is my consciousness for my personality that endows my necessary individualism with its evident sovereignty, thereby rescuing it from every appearance of anarchic constitution. My Pestalozzi cried, "Man, it is within yourself, it is in the inner sense of your power, that resides nature's instrument for your development."

Feeling and wording my self as my one and only one provides me with the motivation necessary to love my neighbor *as* my self and, thereby, to appreciate all of his behavior, no matter how consciously shortsighted and seemingly disregardful, as being absolutely his only accessible way of living necessary self activity. Without this scope of my personal identity I cannot read my morning newspaper with lifesaving equanimity, but rather must suffer the natural consequence of inhibiting my conscious self love when I condemn *my* (impersonated) fellowman. Hence, I frequently exercise the truth that all of my wording of my mental operation is merely my private showing of my self activity. I record my medical psychology? True enough. Aristotle felt, "The Philosopher should end with medicine, the Physician commence with philosophy."

INTRODUCTION

Man need not bend to linguistic circumstance
but may easily bend language to his needs.

Joshua Whatmough

For many years I have observed in my study of "the" literature, *my* literature, that is, instance after instance of my
author's deploring and delighting in the power of words to
conceal as well as reveal the nature of the human mind. I have
also derived great satisfaction from my research upon my fellowman's rare heroic efforts *to try to do something about it,*
for I do consider my way of using my wordage to be a most
important consideration deserving my greatest personal concern.

Conventional "scientific study of language" called linguistics, as the plurality of the name implies is, by and large, the
scientific linguist's effort to understand verbal "communication
between communicators," *objectively.* Thus "descriptive linguistics" is termed "one of the most rigorous and best defined
of the social sciences."

N. Chomsky with a new, generative conception of grammar,
conceives how syntax could provide a common ground for collaboration between linguist and psychologist.[1] A linguist's
"competence" is his knowledge of his language; his "performance" is his actual application of that knowledge when it is
indicated.

Whether I am writing or reading, speaking or listening, I am
equally the *active* linguist, a truth to be borne in mind for my
estimate of my linguistic economy. Certainly, it is of inestimable
advantage for my creating (interpreting) accurately my auditory
experience (e.g., my hearing my fellowman speak, to his self, to
be sure) if I can appreciate what appears to be the specific emotional bias motivating it.

---

[1] *Aspects of the Theory of Syntax,* Cambridge, Mass.: M.I.T. Press, 1965.

xvii

Ever since my self analysis enabled me to honor sufficiently the basic truth of my own inviolable individuality, my writings have recorded my deep feeling about the specific consequence for the welfare of my mankind of each person's gradually assuming his due *word responsibility*. Now I have reached the feeling that *self language study* is my (including my every fellowman's) most critically needed self discipline and that, first things first, it deserves to be considered and heeded as number one curricular concern by every responsible self educator of each level of formal, scholastic, self development. All of my peace derives from the facilitating psychology of revered individuality; all of my war derives from the inhibiting psychology of ignored individuality. My American self government takes on the seeming of mob rule to the extent that I do not work up my appreciation for it as my very own.

However, to proceed wisely in this self reality discipline it is necessary that I fully honor my helpful delusional system called "communication" with which it works. *To be sure, my new growth of self awareness in my language is in no sense any kind of an indictment against my former language helpfulness but rather a development based gratefully upon it. My awakening to feel my self in what formerly did not seem to be my self is the orderly sequence that is integral to my cultivation of my conscious self identity.*

I would not take the trouble to try to "do anything about" my observing the delusional nature of established language were it not for the fact that, unheeded, it tremendously detracts from realization of the greatness of man. All of my appreciation for the magnificence of my "external world" is maintained at the terrible cost of my consciously appreciating my own life. Since every mind must invent its own language, it is justly life affirming that it claim credit for it. I can never find my mind comprehensible without discovering its language to be all and only about it. Disciplining my mind to use its idiolect consciously, as such, is my one sure way to recognize and honor my life affirming self love.[2]

[2] See, "Language of Sanity," *Illness or Allness,* Detroit: Wayne State University Press, 1965, pp. 44–81.

Insofar as each of my words would not consciously consist of my own vital emotionality I would have to describe it as making up a dead language. Only a life *can* give life to any sound.[3] This book records the results of my difficultly discovering and acknowledging my use of established or received language chiefly to support my vast systematized delusion of objectivity, or materialism. First of all, every word of impersonal vocabulary purporting to enable communication is a symptom of my unrecognizable emotive individuality, and is not an enjoyable naming process designating and honoring elements of my conscious self activity.

This little volume is not written expressly for the trade although to be sure, adequately understood, it can but consciously benefit my popular book publisher, seller, and reader. Specifically, it certainly does not, and cannot, detract in any way from the pleasure and profit accruable from whatever kind of best seller, escapist, or objective literature, all of which may be read, enjoyed fully and experienced helpfully by the keenly self conscious reader. Feeling my self in all of my language can only contribute to my self gratifying appreciating that I create my every kind of literature or lecture.

I raise this particular point on account of traditional objection made to any calling of attention to the necessity for a mind's subjectivity, namely, that it is the opposite of objectivity, and hence rules out objectivity. The truth is that my *subjectivity* cannot rule out anything except by ruling out that "anything" only in my subjectivity's own being. Although my objectivity cannot subsume its "subjectivity" my subjectivity can and must subsume all that it can mean by its objectivity. Every man is the measure of all that *he* can consciously mean by humanity, or divinity. His only possible way to unite *his* fellowmen is through his working up his own self's conscious unity. My conscious insistence that (my) anybody else behave in a given way is always traceable to my resisting awareness for my own inviolable individuality by withholding my full apprecia-

[3] See C. Waller Barrett's Introduction to *The American Writer in England*, Charlottesville: The University Press of Virginia, 1969, pp. xiii–xxxv.

tion for *my* fellowman's inviolable individuality. Quite as Leibnitz asserted in his *Monadology*, man makes his own world as he creates his perception. Everyone's sense of self love is the product of his self awareness, however, and conscious being is not the same as unconscious being.

My every word that I consciously originate as an element of my acknowledgeable idiolect, whether it be an article or a sesquipedalian substantive, gives me desirable literary pleasure. I always enjoy discovering its historic origin and development.

I would like to be able to know (to know where to find) the approximate date when, and the exact name of the person by whom my *every* word was first invented. Certainly I always appreciate it whenever I do provide this satisfaction for my self.

I am the only word-stuff of all of my diction, as of all else of my mind, but I can easily lose my feeling of conscious selfness in my own linguistic structure, such as figure of speech or any aesthetic effect of my linguistic or nonverbal functioning, for all of my activity is constantly meaning (emoting) its organic unity in lyric, epic, dramatic, or even silent psychogenesis. Sigmund Freud's discovery of the language of the dream sheds light upon the whole range of linguistics. He developed deepest insight of archaic dream work as having its counterpart in the development of language and thought. Quite as my dream of sleep might represent the survival of the mental activity of my prehistoric ancestor while awake, so my established language of the present may well represent dream language of the future when my fellowman shall have discovered the lifesaving benefits of his disciplining his mind-awake to full appreciation for all of its language as being its *conscious idiolect*.

However, my need to feel consciously lovable is equated with my wish to live and therefore in my mind-awake I resort to the same ways I use to protect my mind-asleep from excitation that is unpleasing. I refer to *dream work*, the wonderful discovery of my Professor Freud. Not merely in my acknowledgeable day dreaming do I follow my wishfulfilling mental functioning but also during what I ordinarily consider to be my wide-awake living. *Only when my mind devotes itself to the functioning of its self consciousness is it fully awake to itself.* However, while claiming to be wide awake without activating my self consciousness, I resort to displacement, condensation, regard for representability, symbolization, use of opposites, regression and even secondary elaboration, in order to change my unconscious feelings and thoughts into the pattern I am *accustomed* to name waking mentation. I have demonstrated clearly to my self my use of sensation and perception as forms of illusion and hallucination, when I do not fully recognize the complete subjectivity of those vivid self experiences. My inability to feel my self, and thus locate my self, in all of my functioning of my senses amounts to a form of daydreaming.

Although my experiences have persistently showed me my habitual use of language as a kind of cover for protecting my mind's *status quo,* I continue to be startled by occasional sight of my elaborate verbal defenses against appreciating that I am whatever I live with dislike, quite as I am whatever I live with love. I am sanest when I can comprehend my vocabulary as a word-picture of my immediate mental situation, thus seeing my every pejorative or meliorative as a helpful resistance sparing my faultfinding self's confronting its intolerable truth that there can be nothing possible to live but perfection. *All* negation, or denial, treats the conscious as unconscious. It is impossible to deny or negate whatever I live consciously.

The more primitive the person, the less he is conscious for his wholeness and the more reluctant is he to speak his name at all. How understandable one's resistance therefore to recognizing his *every* word as a self naming only! According to Sir James George Frazer's account, if asked his name, the primitive Ojibway found a bystander to answer. His reluctance was presumed to arise from the idea he developed as a child that if he repeated his own name it would prevent his growth and make him of small stature. My North American Indian fellowman originally considered name to be a vulnerable part of nature.

The implication of conscious self responsibility for health is sun clear: the sanely developing individual must courageously find it possible to help his growing awareness so that he can keep calling his soul his own and all of his growth his sufficing soul. It is not magic if by thinking constructively, I grow strong and well; or, if by thinking negatively, I grow weak and unbeseeming. It is not magic if by practicing self devotion I develop my powers, or, if by practicing self sacrifice, I obscure my integrity. It *is* easy for the unafflicted to make theories.

However from personal experience I know that it is impossible for me, including my reader, to acquire wisdom that my stage of mental development itself does not immediately require. In *The Friend, II,* language-wise Samuel Taylor Coleridge wrote along this line:

> Mankind in general are so little in the habit of looking steadily at their own meaning, or of weighing the words by which they express it, that the writer who is careful to do both will sometimes mislead his readers through the very excellence which qualifies him to be their instructor; and this with no other fault on his part than the modest mistake on his part of supposing in those to whom he addresses himself an intellect as watchful as his own.

My etymology, a language discipline man began over one hundred and thirty years ago, is the study of my word through written records of preceding years up to the present, until I recognize its origin, all of it, in its only real base for me, in my own self-bred mind. My language is at my mercy only, to use either pretentiously as applicable to another or magnificently as applicable to my wonderful world of self. The original meaning of Satan was: irresponsible groundlessness, turning accusatory. The essential plot of the Book of Job, well regarded as the supreme achievement of wisdom of man, concerns the holiness in Job's devotion to his belief in the adequacy of his own will to be ideally just, without relying upon so-called *external* divine support. Every man is a law unto his self, and his first discovering and then obeying his law is his way of loving, living wisely. He can find it just to use his mind to imagine his soul's identity, divinity, in the whirlwind or whatever wholeness of his world of being.

Self love is specifically life affirming. But my self experience is often such that it is impossible or difficult to associate it with evident love. Even though I may be able to intellectualize that whatever is lived is lovable, that love of life includes all self preservation, nevertheless my pain (including every kind of unhappiness) can helpfully usurp my consciousness pending my disciplining my self to behave with such conscious responsibility that my exciting my lifesaving danger signal of unhappiness becomes no longer biologically indicated.

Sigmund Freud's genius recognizes fear as being the form taken by inhibited wish, "every fear" corresponding "to a former wish which was . . . . repressed."[4] He also sagely discerned that whatever need is inhibited in its conscious functioning become thereby "repressed" to its unconscious functioning of its precisely contrary need. Thus consciously inhibited love itself becomes unconsciously uninhibited hate; consciously inhibited innocence itself becomes unconsciously uninhibited guilt; consciously inhibited longing itself becomes unconsciously uninhibited anxiety; and so on.[5] Only full consciousness reveals self identity in affect.

Whenever functioning of my conscious subjectivity is inhibited, it itself becomes unconscious in uninhibited functioning I call "objectivity." Consciously subjective William Hamilton records: "To create, is not to make something out of nothing, for this is contradictory, but to originate from self." Of the terms subjective and objective he writes:

> The exact distinction of *subject* and *object* was first made by the schoolmen. . . . These correlative terms correspond to the first and most important distinction in philosophy; they embody the original antithesis in consciousness of self and not-self—a distinction which, in fact, involves the whole science of mind; for psychology is nothing

[4] "A Case of Obsessional Neuroses," Vol. X, *The Standard Edition of the Complete Psychological Works of Sigmund Freud,* London: Hogarth Press and Institute of Psychoanalysis, 1955, p. 180.
[5] John M. Dorsey, *Psychology of Emotion,* Detroit: Center for Health Education, 1971, p. 13.

more than a determination of the subjective and the objective, in themselves.[6]

My study of my fellowman's historic effort to work up knowledge of the understanding of human experience according to his genius and ability is a fascinating one, beginning as it apparently did with whatever seemed "inhuman" (e.g., divine, impersonal, remote). Then episodically my historical colleague refers specifically to so-called human nature, also later even to particular human individuality. Only at last does he deal exclusively with all that can be valued as directly real, namely, his very own experience helpfully termed mental. For all of this course of my study I must rely thoroughly upon whatever appreciation for the nature of my language I can muster. The controversy between Nominalist and Realist featured the role of language in my colleague's endeavor to find his sense in his experience.

The Scholastic nominalist (Roscellinus, eleventh century) held that every collective term such as man, horse, thing, tree, cloud, city, and so on, could have no "real, objective existence" corresponding to it, being merely a "vocal utterance, word or name." He asserted insightfully that only particular individuality exists, hence mind cannot justly frame any concept or image corresponding to such a universal or general term. Three centuries later mind observant Occam discriminated between logical, real, and grammatical usage of a word, upholding the principle: Entities must not be multiplied unnecessarily.

John Locke (1632–1704) studied scholastic philosophy at Oxford in a way that sharpened the native genius of his speculative sensibility. While at Oxford he also studied his mind in medicine distinguishing his introspective self as a medical scholar. Subsequently he cultivated his conscious individuality along the demanding lines of his political experience. Thomas Jefferson lived his John Locke's political wisdom helpfully

---

[6] *Discussions on Philosophy and Literature,* New York: Harper and Bros., 1868, p. 13.

while originating his truly wonderful linguistic creation, the Declaration of Independence.

Locke's "Essay on Human Understanding" reflected his fresh look and independent study of his own mental operation, earning for him the title, "Father of Modern Psychology." This essay was started in 1670, completed in 1687, and published in 1690. Self reliantly he courageously observed with vital verbal force:[7]

> First, I shall inquire into the *original* of all those ideas, notions, or whatever else you please to call them, *which a man observes and is conscious to himself he has in his mind;* and the ways whereby the understanding comes to be furnished with them.

I need my wide-awake creative mind, practiced in self conscious reading, to find my sense and own it in my Locke's Essay. Each of my historical readers naturally found fault with it wherever he could not find his self in it. Such is the understandable destiny of all literature. Whatever is, can mean nothing except its own perfect existence. I can exert only my own private mind to measure speculatively my fellowman's mind. All of my intellectual curiosity is helpful self interest. I must be a pupil of no school as well as a founder of none. Genuinely conscious of his own mind in his essay "Nature" (1836), Emerson worded his living language, "The world is a divine dream, from which we may presently awake to the glories and certainties of day."

In the sense that my continuous living is a constant growing of my innovating self in an ever dynamic rather than static constitution, I am never of quite the same make-up in two successive moments. Therefore, I can never even use the same word to say exactly the same thing (think) twice in succession. My imagining I can thus ever be other than original however accounts 1) for my strong illusion of repetition, as well as 2) for my need to use seeming repetition, on account of its really being (instead) always the consequence of my new motivation

---

[7] My italics.

for new experience. This truth explicates fully my use of all my senses to seemingly repeat my self. Thus I enjoy hearing, speaking, reading, writing, etc., over and over again in (only) apparently the same old way.

Since all my language can ever really do is name my self in one emotional aspect or another, I might well make peace with this necessity, particularly on account of the specific helpfulness it only can provide for my discovering the full measure of truth about the wonderful value of my living. It is only expectable that my reader object to confrontation with unpleasing truth in his life that he has accustomed his trusting self to ignore, so that he might not be forced to attend to his painful, unhappy, feelings. However, the old saying, What I do not know, cannot hurt me, does not state the whole truth. What I do not know, can and does hurt me, but I am not aware of that dangerous condition. Hence it is, my hurting experience can imperil my life without my knowing anything about its existence. My reader who seeks distraction from the fact of his wholeness and allness must resist even occasional references to the providence of self consciousness. This *Psychology of Language,* intentionally self relevant only, concentrates upon its author's discovery of the lifesaving importance in his practicing awareness for his inviolable individuality.

My vigilance in acknowledging my total responsibility for my self world has been specifically rewarding in my gaining control of my tendency to fall idly into my stereotyped, conventional, stock language. In this sustained effort I help my self most pointedly by making sure that my word reflects my strong controlling sentiment: emotional self continence.[8] As my Cardinal Newman stated of his Aristotle's magnanimous man, "His language expresses not only his great thoughts, but his great self." To my objection that my constant self reference is redundant I promptly reply, this personal pleonasm is preferable to seemingly foreign neoplasm. I am self eloquent either directly (consciously) or by circumlocution (unconsciously).

[8] *Psychology of Emotion,* p. 85 et seq.

The intention of this self study is merely to record for my self certain considerations supporting one fact: the only reality of anyone's linguistics is his own psychic reality, education in conscious mindfulness fully accounting for his "native love of reality" (Emerson). I have tested and retested this specific significance of self feeling and have asked my fellow scientists to test and re-test it, and it *always* stands the test. My every word-act either reveals me, or conceals me.

All of my use of words to assure my self that I am living in an external world is my pure self delusion maintained at the enormous cost of my biological truth that all I name "external world" does and must exist *only* in me. My choice of diction leads me into conscious fair-mindedness or unconscious fanaticism.

When I am not aware that all of my wording is a creation of and in my own mind only, then my language can no longer describe me so that I can recognize that I am in my right mind. As the gap between my conscious self identity and my imagining my whole external world widens, I become increasingly resistive to thorough examination of my use of words and fierce in my defense of my developing my unconscious living at the expense of my already *acknowledgeable* self responsibility. Numerous then are my signs and symptoms indicating my limited life appreciation, but I must not understand them as disguised helpfulness for that would disturb whatever conscious self identity I have already worked up for my self. I must preserve my conscious *status quo* quite as I do my wish to live.

Although science of linguisitcs seems to have had its recognized beginning in the nineteenth century with the works of Johann Gottfried Herder (1774–1803) and August Schleicher (1821–1868), from the beginning of *conscious* psychological speculation such questions as the following have aroused self observant man's interest. Is my world really the best of all possible worlds, and my inability to realize and appreciate that existing fact merely my best way of avoiding overwhelming responsibility for my world? Can it be far more to the point of my speech psychology for me first to heed that my every word is nothing but my own mind's linguistic love, than for me to seem to forget my self in my fascinating research that does not even seem to be self-ward?

It is always self respecting to honor the term consciousness for its true import: *self consciousness.* However I rarely find literary practice observing this distinction. Rather, literary mind tends to use the words classic and romantic specifically to name contrasts such as 1) societal, static, finished, complete, typical, and 2) individual, dynamic, spontaneous, developing, unique.

My history of human nature is replete with painful lessons of man's effort to help his self in the only way he could, namely, by growing new helpfulness at the expense of condemning his former helpfulness. Thus man's romantic movement, the eighteenth century aestheticist's noble effort to advance the validity of the individual's (subjective) experience, tended to belittle his former practice of subordinating his self to his prevailing classical (so-called objective) forms. Instead of honoring his earlier classical self development for its true worth as the foundation of his further self growth into conscious self appreciation (romanticism), the critic condemned it. The inevitable consequence is evident in illusional classical-romantic duality continued to the present day.

The classicist wrote upon themes other than his own conscious self; the romanticist undertook conscious autobiography. True, the neoclassicist turned to mature man rather than to so-called impersonal nature. However, the romanticist invested his interest in his own personal growth thereby gradually discovering the life-directing importance of his infancy, childhood and *his* natural world. The neoclassicist defined art as the imitation of nature; the romanticist, as the self-creation of the artist's own nature.

John Keats immortalized the ideal of *all* mental development in his beautiful word-picture of poetry: "if Poetry comes not as naturally as the Leaves to a tree it had better not come at all." Romantic, imaginative Byron claimed he would not take the trouble to revise his wording: "I am like a tiger; if I miss my first spring, I go grumbling back to my jungle." Romanticist Wordsworth consulted his inmost sensibility, and purposefully wrote mostly of his self. He considered art to be "the spontaneous overflow of powerful feelings."

My psychology of language scores the lifesaving benefit to me in 1) my feeling my every word as entirely, and nothing but, my own self activity and, therefore 2) my trying to take pains to use my words consistently for naming consciously positive, constructive, life supporting developments in all of my experience.

Throughout my lifetime, beginning with my first schooling, I have always centered my personal and professional study upon my academic educational base. I devote lively interest to my educational process as such, perseveringly developing and testing my feeling about so-called formal schooling, particularly as contrasted with consciously independent discipline in developing self knowledge.[9] As a result of this systematic experience with my process of self enlightenment, *purposively to cultivate adequate appreciation for my life itself,* I feel deep conviction about the absolute necessity that I watch my language as carefully and caringly as I do all of the rest of my locomotion. The importance of philological study for the cultivation of my sanity is primary and profound. I can ignore it only at the most grievous cost of my healthful happiness. It is a lifesaving subject for my lasting rather than occasional concern. Institutions never read or write, speak or hear, blanch or blush.

My so-called mother tongue (including hearing) enters into my habit of mind from birth on, and it is most essential that I try to conceive a philological and grammatical sense of my "baby talk" however difficult and imprecise that certainly must be. Exertion to reconstruct as best I can habitual vocabulary and grammar of my early childhood is also well spent. My later feelingful wording for my school, church, and neighborhood experience can reveal early developments of that precious

[9] In 1925 at the University of Iowa State Psychopathic Hospital, with George S. Sprague, M.D., I began working up clearly personal definitions of scientific terms.

construction I name "conscious self identity." As a professional educator I feel duty bound to mention the obligation I feel to study carefully the written records of my so-called public school administrators, notably the publications, including official reports, of that great American, William T. Harris, justly renowned United States Commissioner of Education, 1889–1906. Godsmith Emerson said of men who find life great and good, "We call our children and our lands by their names. Their names are wrought into the verbs of language. . . and every circumstance of the day recalls an anecdote of them."[10]

I can discover no way at all to educate my self to value and cherish my life except by making my self *keep realizing* that it *is* mine, all mine. It is the power of my language either to reveal or conceal the truth that I am being (doing) all of my own living. I can practice growing and using my vocabulary either to serve or neglect my self recognition and self preservation. I conceive the extensive diffusion of individual life appreciation in my world to be the requisite of intensive cultivation of language honoring each linguist's sole richness and power, his possession of his life. As a linguist I can be only the unremitting, original neologist of my own psychic living.

Innumerable are the temptations to cultivate erudition that in no way seems to designate or even demonstrate the student's own growing of his self realisation. My self ignorance or self erudition as a professional educator can function most powerfully and extensively either to encourage or discourage devotion to conscious self fulfilment in each of my students. I have never observed a student insusceptible of this self regeneration, namely, his renewing his birthright principle of experiencing his living as being his own. The great end of my life is conscious self fulfilment, and it is complete only when I include self awareness in my living. Only living, itself, can be significant. I know of no greater mental exercise than my study of how my mind works its self, and for this science I need my conscious idiolect.

---

[10] See Cecil Hunt, *Word Origins: The Romance of Language,* New York: Philosophical Library, Inc., 1949.

However, the abiding truth that my own life is *all that can be worth knowing* must be respected by me or else I must develop signs and symptoms of my life endangering self neglect. No classical or contemporary erudition can elucidate for me what the law of my nature requires, namely, loving esteem for the wonderful value of my own being. My language as a learned theologian must be recognizable by me as a language of my self, to deliver it from the necessity to be symptomatic of my self disregard. To be a competent divine is, in truth, to be a competent self scholar. My true philological erudition derives from beloved knowledge of my own branded being, the necessary enthusiastic condition of conscious solipsism. Truth is the property only of individual mind. My psychology can be only my study of my individual mind's use of its verbal truth.

Immediate consciousness for all of the selfhood I have grown for my entire individuality, would involve me in overwhelming responsibility for my expenditure of all of my psychic energy. Instead, for my developing my being I have concentrated my consciousness into a focus upon each presenting self experience, thus gradually succeeding in appreciating the vital power of my wholeness. However, I must heed that I am all that I have been, in order to avoid becoming a man in "disunion among himself" (Heinrich Heine).

To rescue from pejoration my word "selfishness" and recognize it as "the stone the builder rejected" in my building of my individuality, has been necessary in order that I make my life ideal, one of self devotion rather than self sacrifice. All of *my* so-called selflessness must be nothing but another growth of my selfness. Plotinus frankly described Nature as "philotheamon," greedy in beholding herself.

In 1804 Friedrich Froebel (1782–1852) invented the word Kindergarten to name his educational center wherein the very young pre-school child could exercise his joy of self consciousness, stating,

> What does the word *German* (Deutsch) signify? It is derived from the word *deuten* (signifying, "to manifest"), which designates the act by which self conscious thought is clearly manifested outwardly. To

be a German is then to raise one's self as an individual and as a whole, by a clear manifestation of one's self, to a clear consciousness of self. . . . It is the greatest mistake to suppose that spiritual, human perfection can serve as a model in its form. This accounts for the common experience that the taking of such external manifestation of perfection as examples, instead of elevating mankind, checks, nay, represses its development.

I find it most helpful to make my diction reflect that my self development is my only possible self activity. In no other way can I escape fitting my St. Augustine's description, "trafficker in words," or my Kant's word-picture, "a pack horse of Paranassus," or Rabelais's account of rote learning as an "abyss of knowledge." By schooling my self in self consciousness I am escaping the delusion that reasoning (itself all rationalization) is my highest mental function. Ignorance recognizable as self ignorance is the desirable appetite of my beloved genius; knowledge unrecognizable as self knowledge is the reasoning stuff of my beloved ignoramus.

In *Psychology of Emotion* I made as much as I could over my life empowering consciousness for the ubiquitous autonomy of my truthful wholeness. Whenever I do not consciously work my wordage I thereby force it to seem to be able to work me, —thus obscuring my appreciation for the *holistic* quality of all of my integrable functioning. To illustrate, my feeling of recognition (including memory), wit, identity, synthesis of any kind (such as Aristotle's "Knowledge of opposites is one"), problem solving, completion, definition, or every such unifying association, is satisfying since it spares my mind the necessity to maintain its illusion of plurality at the expense of enjoying its congruent integrity *in statu nascendi*. I *wholly* am *all* that I ever am, and any of my doing (such as seeing, hearing, speaking, or other acting) is merely my living of whatever I am.

Life-giving pleasure I enjoy from my feeling my wholeness can be disregarded (including, taken for granted) only at the fearful cost of conscious appreciation for my life itself. Lifesaving imagination can unite all with all, thus restoring natural order otherwise constrained in language habit, grammar, nominal specialization, division, and the like. By "natural order" here, I refer to earliest mentality, as found in sleep, free association, dream, joke, art, delusion, delirium, —technically named "primary process."

With regard for the topographic, dynamic and economic dimensions of my psychology of language, each is a growth process, an integral individuation of the development of my whole organic nature. My declared inviolable individuality scores my constitutional autonomy. By definition my individualistic psychic economy is conspicuously a so-called capitalistic one, my every kind of collectivism being readily recognizable as purely illusional plurality. My absolutely solipsistic mentality is necessarily a capitalistic process of my subjectivity. But either consciously or unconsciously I must spend my living in the realistic economy of the best interest of my whole self. In his consciously authored account of Man's divinity, or God's humanity, *The Shining Stranger*, Preston Harold (pen-name) courageously records,[11] "In simple truth, *man cannot escape capitalism for he, himself, is capital-good*. Thus, to take a dispirited view of capitalism is to take a dispirited view of man."

Throughout all of my living I am persistently tempted to feel and name my personal identity in whatever of my living I can enjoy, but to withhold my feeling and name of my personal identity from whatever of my living I cannot enjoy. How such a mind dissociating device for living prevents me from appreciating my congruous wholeness is obvious. Only when I can find my pleasure also in the hard work of acclaiming my difficult life ordeals as entirely mine can I begin to divine and name my every such trying experience as preciously, selffulfillingly, integral to the completeness of my whole, intact being. This disciplined growing of my hardihood is what I call consciously successful living. I find its unifying force essential for my feeling single identity in my hell below and heaven above, in swear and prayer.

[11] *The Shining Stranger.* New York: The Wayfarer Press, 1967, p. 369.

My limit of *conscious* self identity is also the limit of 1) my conscious life appreciation and 2) my conscious volition (will power). Only by arduously and steadfastly extending the limit of my conscious personal identity can I live so that my living is a real profit to my self, including *my* fellowman.

My theme, or working idea, is: the lifesaving helpfulness I find in my honoring my vital unity, wholeness, and allness in all of my linguistic functioning. It formulated itself as I continued to discover my self consistency in my verbiage until I finally could assert *all* of it to be subject of and to me. With this self honoring perspective I began to reexamine my linguistic laws from the standpoint of their duly respecting the fundamental law of my being. I soon discovered the vast extent to which I affirmed my wordage at the expense of consciously negating my conscious self worth, including my appreciation for my organic integrity.[12] This book describes my effort to renounce kindly my linguistic habit of trying to trade my inherent life appreciation for my vocabulary naming my life depreciation.

[12] See my *Psychology of Emotion.*

PERSPECTIVE

Language most shows a man; speak that I may see thee.

Ben Jonson

I observe that my idiolect describes my idiopsychology, that my language reflects my way of using my mind. Certainly my mental subsumes my linguistic power. I find that I can reduce my every word to "I," my every number to "one." Therefore, it is my intention to try to make one of my psychology and language, somewhat as did Wilhelm von Humboldt (1767–1835), Jacob Grimm (1785–1863), Johann Gottfried Herder (1744–1803), G. Curtius (1820–1885), Chajim (Heymann) Steinthal (1823–1899), and later Wilhelm Wundt (1832–1920), Sigmund Freud (1856–1939), Franz Boas (1858–1942), Otto Jespersen (1860–1943), Alfred Korzybski (1879–1950), and an ever increasing number of insightful pioneers in both fields. To this end I base my study of linguistics on my psychological facts and my psychological facts on my human *individuality* only (on my generation of my mind's consciousness).

A *conscious* self educator's clearest view of his language is its exclusive helpfulness for the difficult but lifesaving process of extending self consciousness. However, first I have had to feel my truth that my conscious self identity need not remain a fixed quantity. That truth always hurts too. I resisted the fact that I must see *my* author as my self and live *my* reading of his work quite as my authoring it, if I would fully read it. I resisted noticing the truth that I stopped learning how to use my eyes, or any of my senses, as quickly as I could,—certainly stopping before realizing that whatever I sense or perceive is nothing but an addition to that complex unity I call my mind.

Goethe's epigraph to his life story reveals his *insightful* learning: He who is not skinned is not educated. The art of life observation (of self consciousness) meets Alfred North Whitehead's definition of education: "The acquisition of the art of utilization of knowledge." To illustrate, aesthetic appreciation that conscious self knowledge is conscious self power, reveals that the blind search for power over men can be nothing but one's own unrecognized search for self sovereignty. However, as Robert M. Hutchins noticed, "It is hard to think that education is important when the world is on fire; the temptation is to rush out and join the fire department." Whenever my process of *noticing* my selfness once starts, it stops immediately unless I keep it starting.

Psychologist Paul G. Natorp makes his wise self observation that consciousness, instead of being some kind of reality to be investigated by objectively valid methods, is the foundation and condition of all that goes by the name of reality. Certainly what I ordinarily call reality is present only in my conscious mind, which consists merely of my selfness. However, I also attribute reality to all that I can imagine as being in my unconscious living. Honoring this truth is essential for appreciating the wholeness of my marvelous self. Out of constancy of such watchful self solicitude comes a certain important distinction worthy of the most careful and caring consideration of every linguist, namely: any-kind-of-existence is not at all the same as awareness-for-any-kind-of-existence. Furthermore, just as Stephen Paget worded his conscious truth: "once we begin to talk as if the external world were outside our skins, there is no end to casuistry."

The obstinate fact is that I *can* be aware only for my own individuality, but my every experience is a trial of my conscious integrity. My practice of making that point constantly, and not taking it for granted, is the centering principle of the present work. This hard but good and true realization of my own wholeness and allness enables me to understand that awareness for existence is always and only the perogative of the given existent, that my taking for granted that my awareness can subsume anyone or anything but my very own being is an extravagant investment of my imagination. In his writing career, life-wise Goethe used as his guiding principle, not how to serve "society as a whole" but always how "to increase the substance" of his own personality. Necessarily, I am my only

2

possible reason for living. Job-like I can build reliably upon my conscious self love, be honest with my self, honor my belief in my own divinity by cherishing the integrity I name "my life." "I am not my self," accurately describes my seeming to "lose my mind."

Regardless of how limited is my living that I can consciously claim is mine, whatever extent to which I *can* name my soul my own measures the very foundation of my acknowledgeable natural mind. Hence it is I tend to name unnatural any of my experience that I cannot recognize as entirely my own living. However, naturally I must continue to concern my self with any of my existence I officially reject in the name of not-self. Rudolf Carnap thus formulated *the condition of clarity:* becoming clear as to what is the subject of one's talking and thinking. Until I see it is my self, my subject cannot be clear. Responsibly identifying every content of my consciousness with my individuality only, is a semantic achievement of first consequence for my reality testing. All of my theorizing is *my* practice of it; all of my practice is *my* practical theory. The statistician's way of accounting, ever ignoring individuality, began in the seventeenth century and has flourished ever since.

Warner Fite carefully noticed a dangerous tendency in careless (self unconscious) use of language, "For one who knows no language but his own the correspondence of words and things is an assumption almost inevitable." He adds that learning a foreign language "wrenches the word loose from the thing; it also introduces what is for me the most characteristic product of philosophic reflection: namely, a consciousness of the variety of human points of view."[1] Whoever uses the vital word, ipseity, or selfism, or solipsism? Goethe's paradox, whoever knows but one language knows none, brings out the enrichment of one's present understanding to be attained from growing additional *conscious* self experience.

My self, seeking for its principle of inviolable individuality in everything of my world, thus discovers its helpfulness

[1] "The Philosopher and His Words," *Philosophical Review,* Vol. XLIV, No. 2.

(including its goodness-beauty-and-truth). Meister Eckhart similarly extolled his self orientation as *Istigkeit*. Finding my personal identity in any of my living is all that can satisfy my "passion for parsimony" (William James). How economically A. B. Johnson accounts for the truth of the individual and his illusion of many: "Nature . . . is truly a congregation of individual existences, and language a collection of general terms." Henry David Thoreau wrote in his Journal (February 3, 1860), "When I read some of the rules for speaking and writing the English language correctly . . . I think—

> Any fool can make a rule
> And every fool will mind it."

James Russell Lowell in "A Glance Behind the Curtain" clearly ascribed more force to names than most men dream of: "and a lie may keep its throne a whole age longer" under "some fair-seeming name." In his Journal, May 18, 1832, Thomas Carlyle recorded: "Giving a name indeed is a poetic art; all poetry . . . is but a giving of names."

A person is *always* behaving himself perfectly, ideally, desirably, and powerfully, with or without his awareness for the truth that he is always doing (being) his best. Whatever is, is in its cause always perfectly, ideally, and desirably just. Innumerable are the pettinesses inseparable from necessary ignorance for this open secret. Without this manifest truth to depend upon, any scientist would feel helpless indeed. Its factual orientation, basic for scientist and priest alike, always exists. Vital *awareness* for its existence is the costly desideratum.

Despite my concern for so-called reputability and my willingness to conformity, I can and must conduct my life according to my self confirmed opinion of its whole worth to me. If I wittingly regard myself as a whole self world, I tend to act accordingly; if I privately consider myself a relatively insignificant part of a stupendous whole, I tend to act accordingly; if with awareness I nominate myself alternatingly God or devil or whatever, I tend to act each accordingly. My diction (thought, written, or spoken) tends to regulate my conscious self estimate to an extent far greater than I suppose, unless I constantly cultivate the insight that my every word is all and only my very own viable fluent creation.

Justice O. W. Holmes felt keenly his word's *momentary* existence and application, describing it as "the skin of a living thought" varying "greatly in color and content according to the circumstances." The life of a word is its emotionality and an emotionless word is the result of verbicide. In *Twelfth Night* Shakespeare's Clown declares, "Words are grown so false, I am loath to prove reason with them." My word grows false when I cannot identify my self in it. If I am not in my words there is nothing in them. In *Table Talk* William Hazlitt made the point, "I hate to see a parcel of big words without anything in them." And word economist Emerson plainly felt, "There is no choice of words for him who clearly sees the truth. . . . Any word, every word in language, every circumstance, becomes poetic in the hands of a higher thought." In his *Iliad* Homer saw this unity of speech and speaker, "Whatsoever word thou speaketh, that shall thou also hear." My every word that is not felt by me has an empty sound to it. I am the only neologist of my every term as I am the only semanticist of its every meaning.

My each word facilitates my doing (being) as I please with my mind. And I know of no more potentially life appreciating mental act. In *The Poet* Emerson upheld his tongue, "Words and deeds are quite indifferent forms of the divine energy. Words are also actions, and actions are a kind of words." Well said is well done. I live my linguistic capacity as I do every function, with *all* of my self, —not as a segregated system. I see the essence of my language as an enabling *activity* furthering my joy of living, through satisfying self functioning. Just to the extent that it is composed of words that I cannot own as names for meanings of my mind, I speak only an unconscious language. Just weighing of my words must be in terms of *my* mind's weight. Oliver Cromwell raised this truth, that every word is arbitrary to the individual:[2]

> Words have not their import from the natural power of particular combinations of characters, or from the real efficacy of certain sounds, but from the consent of those that use them, and arbitrarily annex certain ideas to them, which might have been signified with equal propriety by any other.

As in all else, also in language: Whatever word is used, is right. So-called wrong usage always involves the illusion communication implying social intercourse and denying *one-ness of individuality*. Language is made by, in, and for individual man and its only possible social function must be performed only by, in, and for each individual man. In no way can my language be troubled except by my ready habit of naming my sensation, perception, feeling or whatever without my heeding that it is all and only mine.

Whether I use my remote Latin phrase, remorse of conscience, or my nearer English forefather's agenbit of inwit, I verbalize the same feeling. But if I use any terminology without recognizing that it is all and only about me, it does not conform to the truth of my wholeness and allness. My absolute law of language is that it be recognized as applying only to its specific user. For me this dictum is unconditional. My benevolent criticism is acutely needed for protection against the danger of ignoring my self in my use of my words. By watchfulness I am gradually forming my language with the essential element of self feeling in its production, setting at nought any authority other than the innate one I can recognize as my own. My vital vocabulary grows with my development of my range of my conscious imagination (any and all conscious mental freedom). In his *Leviathan* Thomas Hobbes asserted that truth consists "in the right ordering of names." Yet Ernest Weekley notices: Stability in language is synonymous with *rigor mortis*.

My doctrine of the origin of language is that it arises only as

---

[2] Replying to the gentlemen from Parliament officially asking him to take the title of king.

the creation of each individual, to express nothing but self activity, and that it continues in this interest of self activity only (self expression). Socrates helpfully defined a word as a name, and "name" as a compressed sentence signifying: being for which there is a search. My Johann G. Herder and Wilhelm von Humboldt considered the wish and ability to give form to personal experience to be the essence of language.

My every word or expression of any kind that I cannot own as my own creation develops a nature in me, which appears to be other than my own, the prototype of the kind of verbiage supporting neoplasm. Even realizing the naturalness of this consequence, namely, that my self ignoration favors my developing strange body growth in the form of a tumor, I may find it too difficult to practice self consciousness steadily.

All that I can be is whatever I am. I cannot be what I am not. I cannot not-be whatever I am. These consciously solipsistic assertions underlie my amplification of my central sentiment: the specifically unique wholeness and allness of my organic being. The various phrases and sentences I use to advertise my self for my self serve my purpose of *consciously* distinctifying my inviolable individuality for me. That is all that my present writing is about. Although I have tried to attain its spirit, I have hardly been able to live up to Francis Bacon's exacting principle of considerateness for his reader, namely, "knowledge that is delivered as a thread to be spun on, ought to be delivered and intimated, if it were possible, *in the same method wherein it was invented.*"

Throughout my being I feel my exact sameness so that the plan of my book necessarily may seem largely to ignore usual literary devices for attaining the truth of the matter, e.g., unity and wholeness of composition: divisions, subdivisions, headings indicating varying rank of importance, clear skeleton outline, stages of progress, climax, anticlimax, laws underlying interrelations, orders of procedure.[3] To the extent that the literary sentiment may still prevail to say as little as possible about

---

[3] In his *Thoughts,* Pascal noted well: "The last thing we find in making a book is to know what we must put first."

one's self but as much as possible about not-self, I have seemed to commit something of a literary suicide.

In his essay on "Characteristics" Thomas Carlyle makes an assertion that reflects the importance of the wholeness of the individual:

> The healthy know not of their health, but only the sick: this is the Physician's Aphorism; and applicable in a far wider sense than he gives it. . . . Wherever, or in what shape soever, powers of the sort which can be named vital are at work, herein lies the test of their working right or working wrong. . . . In the Body, for example, as all doctors are agreed, the first condition of complete health is, that each organ perform its function unconsciously, unheeded; let but any organ announce its separate existence, were it even boastfully, and for pleasure, not for pain, then already has one of these "false centers of sensibility" established itself, already is derangement there. The perfection of bodily well-being is that the collective bodily activities seem one. . . . Thus too, in some languages, is the state of health well denoted by a term expressing unity; when we feel ourselves as we wish to be, we say that we are *whole*.

It is self consciousness alone that amplifies my consciousness for my wholeness, reflected in my appreciating my mind's becoming ample. I exercise this culminant power of my mind in many different forms of amplification so that it can strengthen itself thereby. Whether in my description, narration, exposition or argumentation my ideal of *conscious,* inviolable wholeness of my individual organic being is indispensable for my recognizing my every literary event as the individuation of that wholeness that it is.

The intentional doctrine of my method of research is as follows: Whatever passes for truth, or fact, or reality with me must be merely *my* truth, fact, or reality. I believe as my consciously great minded William Hamilton (1788–1856) sharply felt, "Fact, —observation—induction, have always been the watchwords of those who have dealt most extensively in fancy."[4] I feel my own conviction in my Hamilton's finding the

---

[4] *Lectures on Metaphysics,* ed. by Mansel and Veitch, New York: Sheldon and Co., 1858, I:53.

8

"study of philosophy" only another term for discovering knowledge of his self, "Unless we can become as little children, docile and unperverted, we need never hope to enter the temple of philosophy."[5] Platonic Socrates, first in feeling his mind as the true realm of all of his observation, thus explicated his divine view, Know thyself!

To attain to a knowledge of my self, I must consciously control my prejudice, passion, and sloth. Rudolphus Goclenius of Marburg in 1594 was one of the first to use the word "psychology." His student Otto Casmann who coined the term "anthropology" also used "psychology" in his publication of 1594. The term was used also by Joannes Thomas Freigius in his published *Catalogus Locorum Communium* in 1575. Charles Bonnet published his *Essai de Psychologie* in France in 1755. By psychology I understand my purposeful systematic study of my mental life, of my conscious subjectivity, of the spirit, soul, or intrinsic self of my whole emotional economy. My word "soul" (and German *Seele*) derives from the Gothic root "saiv-ala," signifying storm. My word "emotion" was originally applied to the upheavals occurring in nature (i.e., in the appearances of an external material world) such as tornado, earthquake, and the like. It is understandable that words for actions of my mind's body would be extended for naming usages of the rest of my mind. e.g., comprehend, understand, reject, air, arm, etc.

To this desired end, of conscious self appreciation for all of my living, I find it most practical to maintain a continuous analysis of my usage of language. And to begin with, I do well to feel real unity in the apparent duality of *analysis* and *synthesis*. As true of every other illusional opposites, although ordinarily treated as two different methods, analysis is integral to synthesis, quite as synthesis is integral to analysis. Each is incomplete without *its* other. There can be no synthesis without the elements of analysis composing it; there can be no analysis without its previous identity in synthesis. Each provides the

[5] Ibid., p. 58.

prerequisite being of its opposite. Furthermore, as William Hamilton carefully cautions:

> The legitimacy of every synthesis is thus necessarily dependent on the legitimacy of the analysis which it presupposes, and on which it founds. . . . But though these operations are each requisite to the other, yet were we to distinguish and compare what ought only to be considered as conjoined, it is to analysis that the preference must be considered . . . a synthesis without a previous analysis is radically and *ab initio* null.[6]

My sustained curiosity about the origin of my language enabled me to discover its source as being the same as all else of my individuality, namely, in my growing it quite as I grow my tongue itself. My first word, as all of the rest of my vocabulary, is only and entirely a self growth of mine. My limited ability in recognizing my every word as my own term referring to my own living only resulted in my inability to realize just where to look for its origin, in my own mind to be sure. However, once I could feel absolutely sure that my every vocable must be my own noise-making self's, I then soon appreciated all of my vocalization as being truly analogous to the self sounds made by my dog, cat, bird, or any fellow creature of mine. After that development I readily cultivated my belief in the underlying identity in my using my voice for 1) freeing emotionality in laughing, crying, grunting, or screaming, and 2) freeing my emotionality in verbalizing it with wordage.

At first I confounded my self with my innumerable words that *seemed* to be able to name anybody or anything but activity of my own mind. Once I started to see through this usage of language as a self screen I could immediately begin to understand my need to create words for naming each element of my mind standing for something or someone in my world of my mind. Only then could I really understand my Aristotle's description of man as a political animal, endowed as he is with the lingual power of nominating all of his world as his wonderful self.[7]

[6] Ibid., p. 70. Cf. the wisdom in the term self analysis or psychoanalysis.
[7] "Language of Sanity," *Illness or Allness*, pp. 44–82.

I may briefly sketch my evolution of my linguistics as first, merely auditory development; later, word play and word magic, followed by formal cultivation of reading, writing and speaking; and only finally emergence into conscious self wording. My inventing my hieroglyph, alphabet, speech, printing, literature, braille (Louis Braille, 1809–1852), and every description of audio-visual living has been my gradual self creation for which I must be fully self conscious in order to be justly proud, and correspondingly life appreciating. My life cannot ever become adequately treasured and cherished by me until I can acknowledge all that it accomplishes for me. Furthermore I can attribute to my fellowman's living only the kind and degree of worth I find and prize in my own.

I get to know about my mind's body first and only later extend my self discovery to the rest of my mind. From the start there are degrees of my knowing anything about my self, it being my tendency to assume that I know my hand, or eye, or whatever, very well when I do not. As a rule I treat my knowing about the use of my senses quite as I do my knowing my fellowman, allowing rather slight acquaintance to pass for sufficient appreciation. Thus when it comes to my being able to see, hear, touch, taste, or smell, my proficiency stops long before I discover that all I can see, hear, touch, taste, smell, or sense in any way must be only and entirely my self.

With regard to my language I assume that I know how to read and write many years before I can even begin to realize that all of my reading or writing must be only autobiographical. Certainly while growing my language I assume I can know what any word means without taking the trouble to know that it can really mean only something about me. Therefore my illusion of communication is steadily indulged and my illusion that I am not all of my own created otherness grows strong with practice. Although I cannot realize then that my language is wholly my effort to verbalize my own self feeling, I can observe with seeming justification that it is the kind of language being used by each one of my family. My mother, father, or sibling, *seems* to be able to communicate, each with the other.

My language can become, in my John Dewey's words, my "cherishing mother of all significance"[8] only when I can exert the irksome effort to recognize it as my idiolect. Otherwise my very own naming propensity appears to be able to lead an independent, double life. All that can really happen in any of *my* experience, with my mother or with *my* anyone or anything else must consist entirely and only of *my* experience. Thus in my seeming to hear her speak to me, I originate my auditory experience of *my* mother's speaking to *her* son while she assumes that he can do her listening for her. In truth, if I want to hear spoken to me whatever my mother seems to say to her son, then I must not only speak such words as she does but also listen to what I am saying. Such is all there can be to so-called communication of the spoken word.

The all-important issue in my education is not so much just how, or why, or when, but rather just *where* it takes place, namely, all in my living of my mind. This distinction is most practical and I make it afresh throughout my work-a-day living for its immediate advantage. That is most useful experience that contributes to appreciation for the wonderfulness of living, and my discovery of my consciousness, including its unconscious operation, has helped me most to this appreciation for my living in its most extensive signification.

It is understandable that as an infant and young child I choose to conduct my life as easily as I can rather than as difficultly as I can, and therefore do not apply my attention diligently or thoroughly as it awakens me to the "embarrassment of riches" I may later come to call my very own self possession. The meaning I gradually grow able to give to my term *individuality* includes uniqueness, unity, and universality, comprehending all that I find my self to be by nature and nurture. The more I can call my soul my own, the more ardently I live my wholeness and thereby proceed justly to make the most of my life. I cannot achieve this lifeworthy self fulfillment by using my language as if it is not entirely subject to, and of, me.

[8] *Experience and Nature,* New York: Norton, 1929, p. 186.

In his *Theaetetus* Platonic Socrates speaks with his Theodorus of the kind of penalty "which cannot be escaped" by those leading a life of injustice:

> There are two patterns eternally set before them; the one blessed and divine, the other godless and wretched; but they do not see them or perceive that in their utter folly and infatuation they are growing like the one and unlike the other, by reason of evil deeds; and the penalty is that they lead a life answering to the pattern which they are growing like.[9]

My self prescribed mental discipline in self consciousness fits Rousseau's dictum, "Obedience to a self-prescribed law is liberty." John Dewey describes freedom biologically as "the release of capacity from whatever hems it in."[10]

Characteristically true to the unity of his "encentric" being, William Hamilton states,[11] "Psychology is only an evolution, by consciousness, of the facts which consciousness reveals." Whenever I am not self conscious I must be self unconscious, that is, my consciousness for my self must be inhibited and required to exist temporarily without my awareness for it. The resulting conscious and unconscious living of self experience does not involve two minds or in any way impair the wholeness of mind. Rather, my ability to concentrate consciously on any of my mental activity depends upon all of the rest of my mind's becoming unconscious. In her excellent book, *Feelings and Emotions*,[12] Magda Arnold discerns the true mental unity in its seeming duality, "The feeling subject feels himself by the fact that he feels his fellow-subject."

It is my feeling of self consciousness with which I save my self from being mad with reasoning. Aristotle describes the philosophic reasoners who "in making reason omnipotent, show their own impotence of reason." The history of my mind of greatest importance is the account of how I used my con-

[9] Trans. Jowett, 3d ed., New York: Macmillan, 1892.
[10] *Reconstruction in Philosophy,* New York: Henry Holt, 1920, p. 207.
[11] *Metaphysics,* I:184.
[12] New York and London: Academic Press, 1970, p. 305.

sciousness either to affirm or deny the allness and wholeness of my personal identity, —not even as much to understand me as to acknowledge me.

In finding my self I find the absolute with which I can then imagine my absolute ideal, universe, deity, or whatever. I cannot feel (including know) anything I do not, my self, experience. This assertion, rather than being a substitute for proof, is itself proof of my conscious being. I am absolutely one and my identity as unity is convertible with absolute negation of difference and plurality. When my self consciousness is most active I feel most alive. The fact that I can be conscious without crediting my self with that power may lead me to assume that being conscious is the same as being consciously conscious.

Whatever mental activity is mine does not constitute the same living as my mental activity that is consciously mine. Thus, I can see, hear, touch, feel, or whatever self activity, without immediately feeling personally at all responsible for creating that specific living. To know *what's what* is might; to know *where's what* is right. I create the nature of all of my externality. When I hypothesize "representation" I resort exclusively to my comforting doctrine of dualism, rather than take the trouble to make conscious room for one of my own mind's innumerable modifications. Truth *is* one, and the purpose of my psychology is to cultivate my intuititon about my unity. Fabled Narcissus mistook self for not-self to "fall" into unconscious self love rather than to *rise* consciously to love his inviolable wholeness and allness.

Every word is a name. A name is all and only a name, whether it designates individual or universal, part or whole, relative or absolute, internal or external, singular or general, and so on, throughout all so-called antithetical terms. This realization resolves the phantom problem created by attempting to trace the earliest origin of wording by arguing whether it was the linguist's effort to utter a proper (individual) or appelative (general) denomination. Individual unity of my homogeneous mind is the composition in which all naming of my action occurs. Definitude is produced by my focusing my attention on any individuation of my individuality, and it is helpful to recognize that *wholeness* is the nature of my every mental event, —sensation, emotion, perception or consciousness.[13]

Aristotle felt this wholeness also in respect to body sensations and feelings of mind (*De Anima*), "the soul is all in the whole and all in every part." The same indivisible living is all that is active in any mental functioning. However, I find hardly anything that can be called scientific or popular literature which does not take for granted the untenable theory that one mind can influence, and be influenced by, another, as if one might deforce or be deforced by another.

[13] See Hamilton, *Lectures*, II: 320–332 and 417–418.

MY VOCABULARY

I teach that all men are mad.

Horace

Every instance of my *growing* my self purposefully to appreciate the whole nature of my intact creaturehood is always a great crisis in my evolution of my sanity. This seeing and feeling the allness nature of my ever inviolable self is never, and never can be, the product of any kind of instruction. Rather *all* of my learning is (and can be) only my own living (growing). True, all of my knowing *is* nothing but my being, but that is not precisely the point at issue.

The fine point at issue is that of the need for lifelong practice of esteem for self consciousness. My language can contribute to my conscious self esteem only if I heed that I create all of it. Acknowledging my self as the free and independent originator of my every word enables me to say what I mean and mean what I say. *Conscious* self knowledge is felt. *Feeling* that I am my only possible subject of remark has all of the advantages of being awake to my self: my using words as if they do not refer only to my self is a definite degree of talking and listening in my sleep. My self consciousness, the only possible kind of consciousness, is never any other kind of educational experience except my life lesson in which only I can be teacher pupil and subject. All of my knowing is my inner living making *itself* knower and known. *Only conscious self knowledge based upon conscious self love can amount to wisdom.* The enlargement and enrichment of my whole ideal of human individuality depends entirely and only upon my mind's clear awakening to its responsibility for being all and only itself.

In helping my self by using my mind for the purpose of some self concealment, I obscure its conscious native integrity. Rather my every word speaks for my mind, quite as does my pronoun "I." No matter how I vivisect my mind (defensively, for the purpose of staying alive and of wishing to go on staying

17

alive), my strictly self containing individuality does *all* of the living of it. My life is not a thing to be divided or multiplied, no matter how I set my words in array, no matter what my vocabulary may seem to take for granted to the contrary.

Rather than enriching my mind with words for unconsciously obeying my dominant traditions, I have found it immensely helpful to learn to speak all over again, this time putting (an invisible or inaudible) "my" before every word I use. Thus divinity becomes felt rather than hearsay. God and worldly good are palpably one. Only in this way can I avoid trading my birthright (my potential appreciation for my conscious wholeness) for a mess of wordage concealing my wonderful world of my unique being. In the sense that foreign language means a language foreign to one's self, every nomenclator of my world can speak only a foreign language; for nearly his every word appears to be a term of someone or something other than (alien to) his self.

Every one being an originative all-one, his language is necessarily an idiolect. Instead of habitually darkening my self counsel with words in which I cannot recognize my own living I need most of all a glossary defining my every word or term I use for, and as, describing my being. Without simulating the vocabulary of any impersonal science, I record in my Glossary certain key words used by my mind for naming its vital processes, and provide some rough definition for each one.

The fact that a word is a name for mental process but not that mental process itself, raises the necessity to observe my act of naming as being itself a unique mental process requiring due consideration.

My language is its own subject. *It* is all and only whatever it appears to name, and therefore it cannot function in some sort of equivalence between its self and some nonlinguistic existent. The feeling in my any word derives from whatever emotion I may happen to be exciting, as in satire or irony. In addition, of course the mood of the reader decides for him what word he wants to use, and how, to such an extent that he will discontinue wording that rubs the wrong way. There is no way for me to become master of my words except by becoming master of my emotion, the master nerve of life.

Acknowledging emotion as the meaning of meaning relieves all wording of the impossible function of communication, and reveals communication as a diluted form of "alien control," like hypnosis, autohypnosis to be sure. My words are meant to be read (created by my reader) only for his private satisfaction. Only one's private interest is the lively extension of his personal identity I call *self consciousness.* My poet E. E. Cummings's publications preserve this privacy admirably. Any poem tests my ability to enjoy my own mind's stirring, not the poet's. Poetry *is* the supreme use of language in that its poet recognizes its existence for its own sake (Archibald MacLeish).

I propose that the process of naming is my proper place to begin featuring my heeding that my every word or term is a synonym for my one and only genetic name, I. My emotional situation decides my word feeling, not the converse. Thus, I may curse pleasantly, revile tenderly, detract flatteringly ("damn with faint praise"), speak love spitefully, and so on, depending entirely upon how I feel, despite what "the dictionary says." My every word's individuality can exist only as a verbalization of my whole individuality and its meaning is a functioning of my whole self's meaning only. Every poet rather expects his language critic to defend established usage in good society against *individualistic* momentary original creativity: convention against invention, intellectualization against passion, explanation against revelation, abnegation against evident self love, intelligibility against strangeness, acquisition against intuition, relationship against identity, literalness against figurativeness, easily attainable dualism (or any pluralism) against difficultly attainable solipsism, (mystic) realism against (real) mysticism.

"I know of no more radical romantic egoism," I can hear my reader exclaim (to his self), "This is too much! Descartes tried something of the kind, confounding human with angelic language and psychology. As you do, he too conceived his 'thinking' to be independent of 'things'—autonomous, innate, intuitive. Thomas Aquinas pointed out this mental power to be typical of angelic thought, not of human thought. Descartes also claimed his understanding to be nothing but his mind's capacity to grow and see itself, quite as you do." All such strong resistance helpfully reveals the strength of what is resisted.

I use the word "I" to designate my whole person, whatever I live consciously or unconsciously. The word "person" designates my identity as a developing human being of unique strangeness, conscious or unconscious. The term spirit names the ideal *subjectivity* that is the true nature of the soul of my life. Spirit is the breath and being surprising all of the reality I am, my life consciousness or awareness for the might and magnitude of my power.

My particular kind of self observation named fact is a specific, fresh, life view that is a help in rendering my thrilling experience understandable. A study of the factuality of my any act or omission will thoroughly indicate its *moving* goodness, desirability and specific helpfulness to the full satisfaction of a consciously just-minded man. This life lesson is one of the most important I have taught my self. Justice is a name for responsible recognition of the truth that fact-finding always leads to the renunciation of faultfinding. A fact or truth is always, exists only, in its making, and is to be explored in its structure of process, in its making itself. A so-called static fact is an afterimage of the dynamic event of the fact's self creation. Producing is the product. Resulting is the result. *The becoming of anything is the preserve of its being.* Every seeming object is merely this real subjective process of its creating itself. Knowledge is the knowing only. It is practiced Hebrew idiom to use the verb with the cognate noun, thus, "I feared a fear."

My only possible use of language being that of nominally distinctifying elements in my own mind, my only use of grammar must be that of distinctifying my varying usages of my language. The Greek use of the middle form locates action in the mind of the meaner. This unique provision for self reference, a distinguishing feature of the Greek language, makes it an ideal word-system for constructing *insightful* education, philosophy and psychology.

Each of my words is not a dictionary word but is rather my mental word. By individuality I mean but one kind of individualism, namely, the absolutely necessary kind imposed by the fact that human being occurs all and only in the form of individuality. The habit of opposing individuality with anything else, beginning with "the collective or corporate body of society," merely illustrates the need for competence to recognize the absolute allness and wholeness of individuality itself.

All so-called uniformity of minds, agreement of thinkers, individual relationships constituting Society, human institutions, organizations, associations, consensus of persons, scientific world and innumerable other terms hypostatizing non-individuality depend solely and wholly and specifically upon the "need for competence" stated above. As John Dewey pointed out, "the intrinsic limit of knowledge is simply ignorance." Of the emergence of new individualism he wrote, "such progress will not be initiated until we cease opposing the socially corporate to the individual."[1]

My mind is a word that distinctifies my self as a distinctifier subsuming that which is distinctified. My word meaning distinctifies each of my mental elements in terms of its emotional usefulness. Meaning is the basic affective unit of my nature I name mind. I mean emotionally whatever I mind. My word "sense" also distinctifies a certain excitability or irritability that I can find to be a property of my living. Generally the sense of personal identity I excite in my sensation or perception may be very weak and even pass unnoticed, but it is always present of course. My word "property" distinctifies something that I own by virtue of being (living) it. My word "discovery" distinctifies an element of surprise in my consciousness, derived from the ever fresh novelty of living.

"Imagination" is a vocable that designates any and all of my mental activity (being). Thus sensing or perceiving is imagined

[1] *Individualism Old and New,* New York: Minton, Balch and Co., 1930.

21

quite as feeling or reasoning is imagined. All of my mind is imaginable, but each of its reals is imagined in a way peculiar to it. As Emerson observed, "We live by our imaginations."

Although "being" names inclusive significance of my mind which exists only in so far as I live it, my mind, nevertheless, may and does from habit posit this term, being, without crediting itself with the valuable fact that its every aspect is imaginable only by my mind. Habit that thus obscures self consciousness resembles first death rather than second nature.

My knowing is nothing but my observing my selfness. *Knowing* is the only form in which my knowledge occurs. Knowing is observing self-fact, that is, something which self is. My empirical data are the facts of self observation created by my life's growing itself. Although my every experience serves further unification of my self, this unification is seldom a conscious one, so that I can hardly avoid attributing seeming disunity to my oneness. My mental process of knowing, cognition (my imagination's making reasoning out of its emotion), is a reality that may exist with or without my heeding it as an existent of my existence. "Life" is a word I use to name my *living* of my comprehensive self possession, my owndom, the only source of my only reality or world or divinity. Newton Arvin wrote:[2]

> It is no accident that, emblematically at least, at the very gateway of American literature should stand two autobiographies: no accident that Jonathan Edwards should have written his "Personal Narrative" or Franklin the story of his life. Nothing was more natural than that Edwards and Franklin should have taken themselves as "subjects." . . . Only one essential note in our national chorus remained to be struck, and that was the secessionist note of the frontier; when Fenimore Cooper created the character of Leatherstocking, the embodiment of backwoods resourcefulness, independence, and idiosyncrasy, the ensemble was complete.

My reader can find this book lifeworthy only to the degree in which he makes it an opportunity to become its author, by

[2] Individualism and the American Writer," *Nation,* 133 (October 14, 1931), 392–393.

22

taking the trouble to *feel* all that there can be in it for him, namely, his own living of it.

The greatness of literature can be determined only by the innate sensibility of the individual mind involved in creating it out of its own solipsistic greatness. I can live neither in a *vacuum* nor in a *plenum*. Whatever I possess in mind regarding either spatial illusion must live only in me and be only of my living.

My word "consciousness" distinctifies my sensing living, my feeling my being alive or a life. *Without self awareness I am without accurate perspective.* Self consciousness is the very principle of my true life affirmation. All of my living is original. Nothing can be derivative. I do not create "the" universe; I create my universe. In living my fellowman, it is the pure culture of his peculiar individuality that I must honor, in and with my self appreciation.

By keeping my mental eye open (exciting my self awareness) through heeding my every word as my self word, I see clearly that I am affirming the worth of life in the only way that I consciously can. My life orientation is one that I must constantly keep creating if I will have it. This particular kind of self culture is the most difficult one, and I am making it my life's work. Walt Whitman heroically emoted, "I will effuse egotism." My development of understanding language as completely and only self relevant may be traced in terms of the development of my self consciousness and its issue, the scope of my comprehension for my personal identity. As my tolerance for my emotionality grew I began to feel the identity of my emotional control and my self control, thus gradually attaining a degree of conscious emotional continence compatible with recognizing my language as my idiolect.

However, everyone of my world who writes about any subject, including language, believes more or less firmly that he thinks seriously enough and is emotionally composed enough to know surely what his every word means. Actually my every word possesses a uniquely variant emotionality whenever I use it, merely seeming to be the same as before. Thus I can involve my self in no end of illusional logomachy. Such a phantom problem can be solved only by my dispelling my illusion that my word lives me permanently, rather than that I live my every word momentarily.

A most important help for me in my trying to live my life consciously as my own is to be aware of the self deception inherent in any and every kind of illusional tangling alliance of my subjectivity with any so-called objectivity. Freedom from every illusional agreement or disagreement is possible only to the extent that such fanciful alliance is seen as impossible. My physics or theology has no probability whatsoever except in the sense of *my* physics or my theology.

By "conscious" I refer to the several stages of my being awake to myself through my sensing-perceiving-feeling-knowing and in every other way imagining the true marvelousness of my existence. Comprehensively appreciated consciousness, consciousness identified by me as self consciousness, is my living in which my being and my heeded being constitute the same single vital act, so that my selfness is fully credited with, and honored for, its wonderful power, perfection and productivity. Only self consciousness constitutes the doing-being that is heeded as a reality of my mind for which to be and to-be-lived-only-by-me are recognized as one and the same self experience.

It is not possible for one element of my wholeness to be in conflict with another, despite innumerable appearances to the contrary. Study of the fact (truth) reveals all so-called conflict to be unrecognized concord. Subjective-ideal-spiritual *I* cannot be in conflict with itself. Nothing can be in conflict with itself. Whatever is entirely is, and an *all* obviously has nothing to conflict with.

My living enables me to create self views, self observations. Every view or observation I make, whether I acknowledge it as my creation or not, passes sentence on what I am ready to live, in what direction of self helpfulness I am all set to devote my attention or interest. My definition of successful living is: my disciplining my mind to observe that it succeeds itself, that its every new experience is a succession of its very own being. My real success is to be able to stay alive, with awareness for that precious staying power. This practice provides me with my emotional exercise in life appreciation, no less. Taking my living for granted is my most dangerous consequence of my self unawareness. I can live nothing which I am not, hence there can be nothing adventitious in my living. I can create the view that it is possible for me to live that which is not my own life, but that very fanciful view is my own creation.

I have devoted hours and hours to the study of my dictionary without consciously realizing it to be an adventure in self discovery. However when I did awaken to my conviction that I am not detachable from whatever I live, including my wording, then I understood all of my language to pertain only to my individuality. My mind is one, and helps itself by seeing its unity in every kind of dialogue or colloquium. First and last for the psychology student to study is his (her) self, thereby developing complete personality. Mind can be only self defining. As all definition can have only self-definition as its ground, all personal experience consists only and entirely of mind defining its self, developing its distinctions. It employs its own language by generating its every term as a new thing (whenever that thing or think functions), as living movement.

Since my use of words merely confers names upon my mind's elements, an element's name is not the element. Each one of my mind's elements is all and only about itself: sensation is all and only about sensing; perception is all and only about perceiving; love is all and only about loving; hate is all and only about hating; fear is all and only about fearing. So-called repeating this truth is lifeworthy exercise.

I, can be aware for living only that which I mind, that is, live mentally. I can live only that which I live presently. I can mind (imagine) my ability to live other than presently, but again, that verbal view is only a creation of mine.

Most extensive well-meaning literary self immolation in my world of writers supports apparently rampant depreciation of the truth of the wonderful greatness and goodness of every individual human being and thereby unwittingly reinforces its every reader's most burdensome health condition: self disesteem. Everyone's recognition of the true worth of his individual human being would establish the one condition needed to give accurate solid meaning to his now premature assumption and claim that he already enjoys the benefits of far-advanced civilization. Furthermore, this specific lack (of the individual's due appreciation for his wonderfulness) may be validated and verified in my fellowman's extreme present need for adequate self esteem. The impossible (except illusional) respect of man for his fellowman cannot suffice, except as an oppressive burden for each one. When this oppressive and artificial load is removed, each can find his own undisguised proper *self* respect, *self* honor. This new man must be a self discovery by the individual (and for the individual) of the marvelousness of his own individuality. He can spread this truth only in his self. In *his* only world of reality he sees his soul as the only possible believer. Aristotle says, "The soul is as it were all the things that are."

There may be little or no conscious idealism in my given scientist's linguistics, although subjectivity is the only solid reality of any subject matter, no cloudland. Nature is the symbol of spirit, —"Visible thought," Heinrich Heine named it. My objectivity-centered scientific approach to language arbitrarily negates its ideality or subjectivity, *thereby* postulating its materiality or objectivity. Thus my "bifurcation of nature" problem arises, which I must solve as did my *identity* philosopher Schelling.

My linguistic study based upon subjectivity uses observation, conscious self observation, as its necessary scientific foundation. But as an externality oriented scientist, I would have to regard such procedure as unscientific.[3] On the other hand, as a conscious self observant scientist, I recognize the real self merit underlying my traditional impersonal scientist's so-called objective work and realize that it is purely subjective whether that scientist considers it such or not.

By my scientific approach, as an insightless (dispassionate) researcher I still mean: striving for the purest possible objectiv-

---

[3] See, Robert A. Hall, Jr., *Idealism in Romance Linguistics,* Cornell University Press, 1963, for an account of the so-called "harm" done by idealism in linguistics.

ity. Thus my scientific language is viewed as a communicable, interpersonal, transitive utterance, not as an intransitive expression of-about-and-for my individual mind. My vocabulary of objectivity is replete with terms meaning my negated subjectivity: space, motion, time, plurality, cleaving, separating, change, coming, going, arriving, departing, conveying, and so on. With my negation of subjectivity-consisting individuality must go my negation of universality. My every "externality" meaning is a symptom of my repressed internality.

As an insightless scientist, I cannot imagine my research, factual investigation, experimental analysis and synthesis, or scientific systematology as a whole to be nothing but my life process. My time-honored opinion of human individuality as one of billions does not enable my conceiving easily its allness-wholeness-and-nowness. My very idea of every person's developing his very own idiolect *ex novo* from his living his self experience of his adult's speaking of *his* own mind—such an idea must be officially condemned as disorderly, insubstantial overestimate of the role of the individual's imagination in creating nonphysical, ghostly immaterializations.

Verification is the essential element of my science. My research is nothing but my verifiable mental living as an individual scientist, disciplined in a given direction of self searching. I give birth to my self observation, experiencing my laboratory for my self generating delivery room. I develop each new fact to fit the readiness of my mind to create such a self development. My research is not a scientific investigation of external objects, but it is my verifiable concern with the being of my own meaning, with my effort to interpret comprehensively my choice of my own selfward mental development. I esteem it as the first known and validatory systematic method of discovery, honoring the tried and true trial-and-error method.

My review of textbooks on education reveals each one consistent in presenting the knowing teacher as imparting essential facts of life to the unknowing pupil by means of interpersonal language "communication." This helpful delusional system is widespread and fiercely defended by administrator, teacher, and pupil alike. The need for its comforting disregard for the individuality of individuality is strong and persistent. It proves to be a blind spot and a sore point whenever it is the subject of consideration. One may well be grateful for it; for it does appear that without it there would be no public school system in anyone's world. *Resistance to the truth must be esteemed quite as much as conscious identity with it.* Without such helpful resistance I would be unable to maintain my appreciation for whatever inviolable oneness I have thus far developed. Also without precious resistance to distraction I cannot focus my attention.

However, one lesson I have taught my self is that the greater any objectionable imagining is, the greater is the corresponding need for it. This realization I learned from studying the forceful facts and by always sufficiently accounting for so-called objectionable conditions of every description.

It might be reassuring to see the textbook of each succeeding generation as clearly reflecting so many stages in the progressive development of author-appreciation for the inviolability of the human mind and its consequential necessity that *it* educate entirely and only itself. But one must forego this source of repose because every author *is* all that he considers to be his own generation, or his preceding or future one. The ancient Greek's word for "I learn" means "I teach myself."

Every kind of knowledge (other than admitted self knowledge) appears acceptable learning because it seems abstractable from its only subsistence, its knower. So-called scientific knowledge is consciously reputed to be information about "the" world as if it could be abstracted from the scientist's personal experience. By "abstracted" is meant: drawn apart from its context, imaginary separation, inattention to the essential element of wholeness in the part. One's processes of abstract mathematics (e.g., such as plural and fraction) are possible through his inattention to his oneness. Thus Emerson intentionally abstracted his very own personal populace: "Every violation of the truth is a stab at the health of human society."

How to renounce indulgence of my linguistic habit of abstracting many a hidden self meaning, such as externality, from my sense of selfness, is my number one health problem. It was not evident for the serious life-and-death issue it really is, until I developed sufficient self coverage in my self awareness to recognize and respect it (this habit indulgence) as a helpful symptom warning me of most dangerous living.

However, once I recovered my mental equilibrium (my vital balance of self respect) sufficiently to heed my habit of self disregard as the important symptom it is, I began to notice the extent to which both my casual and prepared speech disclosed limited mind recognition, which was in turn undermining my conception of my life's value. Against the background of the insight that my every word is my self word, I was startled to see to what extent my speech, both schooled and unschooled, betrayed my necessarily futile efforts at self ignoration, self oppression, self disloyalty, self irresponsibility, self amnesia, self anesthesia, and innumerable other symptoms. All were resorts to countless efforts to dispossess my self of my helpful but painful life experiences.

Shakespeare dramatized, "Mend your speech a little, Lest you may mar your fortunes." My every word signifies the course of my self love, the primary source of my wish to live. I can name only my own love's vicissitudes. All of my language *is* my psychology. In the sense that science is a well made language (Condillac), the biological adequacy of my psychology depends directly upon the extent to which it *consciously* constitutes well made language. It is essential to my health that I work up my ability to recognize my own mind in all of my vocabulary. No one other than my self in my world can ever speak or hear, read or write, my idiolect; and the idiolect of everyone else must forever be foreign to me. Indeed I can never address or be addressed by any of my fellow creatures. Such privacy is the necessary perquisite of individuality. Whatever I live exists for my sake only.

Historically language may have been definable conveniently by monarchical (or dictatorial) man as current verbal coin of the realm for the ready use of the great king or leader and all of his subjects (e.g., "plain King's English, with nothing mystic about it"). Such description, however, hardly answers the onomastic needs of the free man who knows and cherishes that he is all and only his very own subject. William Torrey Harris, conscious American individualist, described his language as "spiritual protoplasm," and asserted that maturity of spiritual development does away with grammatical infections. He admired Emerson's spirited poem, "Brahma," extolling the Hindu's cultivated self insight, and described its stalwart idealism as a kind of antidote for the gorgonizing effect of one's materialistic terminology.

Does my every activity speak to, and for, me, in that it is lovingly self meaningful self activity? As Ernst Cassirer believed, does my own language awareness open "an original phase of spiritual and intellectual life?" All my life endangering experience results from some obstruction to my using fully my own power, quite as all my strengthening and healing is always a welling up of resources for conscious self realization enabling further imaginative appreciation for my own being. Just as did Charles Pierre Baudelaire (1821–1867) I find my imagination to be the most scientific of all of my mental action, all of my discovery of science being a product of my free association, an issue of my life need.*

My only possible influence over my speech is found in my conscious emotional continence. My accurate language of living must be my own conscious soliloquy, and my learning *conscious* language of self immediately functions as ideal practical mindfulness, approximating the Uniate or "wholly the Divine" of Plotinus. As I learn to use my every word while heeding it as my personal living, I need not go on suffering my vocabulary as if it can use me. My mental idiom is a true word picture of my mental condition. I mislead my self by using my word "expression" without realizing that none of me can be "pressed out." The scholastic adage, *individuum est ineffabile,* applies to self definition too. My voice, as impassioned Longfellow said, is "the organ of the soul," and as ardent George Eliot felt, it is "but broken light upon the depth of the unspoken." My wordage changes with all of the rest of my living,

* By free association here I mean: my conscious wording of my uninhibited stream of consciousness.

and my every term is a fixation until I resolve it by sensing its viability. My potentially peaceful idiolect is as uniquely individual as my fingerprints. Little wonder one may be willing to defend his particular use of language even with his life.

Occasionally the question is still posed, When will the scientist *consciously* learn that his mind is his only source of knowledge? The truth is, all that one *can* know is entirely and only about his own self developments. His own mental data on any subject are his only possible data on it. This truth orientation, dormant and unsuspected throughout my early life, has gradually become the foundation for all of my reality. John B. Carroll presents most interesting figures on the tremendous "intake of speech or writing by the average individual," which indicate that a student "could easily be exposed to three-quarters of a billion words a year."[4] And by far most of these words are outright pejoratives or melioratives, valueless for the dictionary consultant's appreciating them as names for elements of his own being, but readily applicable as names for his illusional externality or otherness. Very few words are helpful for calling one's attention to his very own excellence, of which he entirely consists. Most of my vocabulary, instead of constantly reminding me of my true inherent wonderfulness, gives rise to my overwhelming illusion that I cannot really amount to very much compared with the greatness, power, and glory I must attribute only to my external world. Little wonder self scholarly Emerson cried, "Man is the dwarf of himself."

There is a mind orientation that is indispensable for me, including *my* every worker on the alleged level of mental events. I refer to my ever conscious need to localize my each and every function precisely as being in my own mind. Use of words in the effort to objectify my interests, to try to make them appear means of "communing with others" instead of ends serving my own living, is the specific source of unconscious mental dissociation called "mental disorder." Awareness

---

[4] *Language and Thought,* Englewood Cliffs, N.J.: Prentice-Hall, Inc., 1964, p. 2.

31

for localizing all of my wording as being entirely contained in my own being, is the specific vigilance safeguarding my consciously finding, rather than unconsciously losing, my mind in my self educative experience. John Burroughs (1837–1921) defined a man worthy of his name "so long as he preserves his own personal identity, acts and thinks from what is born within him." My being able consciously to nominate my every experience with a name of my own choosing is helpful in my identifying it as being of my being, power of my power. I can recognize my freedom in any of my living that is chosen by me. William Graham Sumner felt.[5]

> It is vain to imagine that a "scientific man" can divest himself of prejudice or previous opinion, and put himself in an attitude of neutral independence towards the mores. He might as well try to get out of gravity or the pressure of the atmosphere. . . . The most elaborate discussion only consists in revolving on one's own axis.

Being entirely local and temporary, here and now, my living naturally requires a vocabulary that can sincerely honor my constant presence by name. My self consciousness is a kind of saving of my life. My feeling that I am being (doing) all of my own living features my appreciation for the power and glory in my immediate self realization. Most important employment of my emotionality is that of duly appreciating what my continent living of it can accomplish for me.[6] This kind of life orientation biologically demands wording that accurately describes my true solipsistic nature.

As my language now stands fixated I find it most difficult to controvert its overwhelming evidence that I am only one of billions, living on earth in an immeasurable universe, sharing the

---

[5] *Folkways,* Boston: Ginn and Company, 1906, p. 98.
[6] *Psychology of Emotion, passim.*

pitiful fate of my equally impotent fellow creatures, and so on and on. Thus I can use my very own words to make my self seem to fit into my own make-believe world of machinery and machination without ever once recognizing it all as a vast delusional system completely of my own making. *I cannot feel the truth that by disowning my mind, I disqualify it for accurate observation.*

To illustrate, my vocabulary of my objective science functions specifically as if it can alienate me from my own self activity. Its wording is selected on the hypothesis that it does not name me personally at all. My objective science assumes the undemonstrable (external reality) as the proving ground for its alleged demonstrability. As a rule this objective science of mine is *felt* to be dispassionate. Although its domain is necessarily the superficial one of surface phenomena, its terminology builds a veritable external tower of Babel. It is a science of magnitude, of quantifiable exactitude, of rigid grammar, —apparently a far remove from the unitary quality of me, its individual and freely growing creator.

My pursuit of this kind of scientific verbiage is perilous indeed. It absolutely incapacitates my mind, inhibiting invigorating consciousness for its only possibility, its self activity. My precise mathematical language, although convertible with the language of self unconsciousness, is not the naming with which my science of my mind can be worded. Although I had to find this truth, as every other one, by my self, my study of the history of my so-called objective scientist reveals him regularly as peculiarly unready for *any* conscious psychological research, especially for any search for the dignity and wonder of his individual mind. My consuming my interest in devotion to my name-giving of objective science turns my attention away from my cultivation of appreciation for my life itself. Thus I become a so-called materialist with no possibility of finding what is the matter with me, and of me.

Although my scientific leaders have long since renounced the very possibility of a philosophy or psychology of so-called materialism, I, including nearly all of my fellowmen, may never discover the importance of that truth in my lifetime. Meanwhile I conduct my life largely according to what my language seems to make of it, my *habit* of wording my mind being to obscure the truth nature of my life's creative spontaneity.

Fortunately, as Plato observed, only the study I force upon my self is ever voluntarily cultivated by me. Purposively disciplining my mind with self consciousness I discover 1) its quality to be entirely personal, emotional, and subjective, and 2) its quantity to be literally and figuratively *one* only. To qualify my mind as somehow quantifiable I may point out that my growth of mental competence depends upon how much of my so-called world I can name and call my own conscious world of my mind.

Word hero Herman Grimm (*Essays on Literature,* 1861) recorded of his esteemed Emerson, "He uses every word in a sense that suits him at the moment, and whether the rest of mankind apprehend it or not is quite indifferent to him. . . . A person appears in a very strange light if he is all on fire with a subject which others regard without the slightest emotion." In his second essay, written after peerless Emerson's death, Grimm noted, "What he has written is like life itself . . . Emerson never wished to say more than just what at the moment presented itself to his soul."

Honoring what is personal and immediate is my only possible way of revering all that I can mean by universal and eternal. However, my language can and often does betray my divinity by appearing to elevate my so-called esoteric knowledge, with the illusive name of education, higher than my knowledge grown as my evident self experience. Thus my very own religious education may be lived by me as if it could be impersonal.

My everyone is, and can be only, an independent, original thinker or feeler, but it is rare for anyone to be able to appreciate this life honoring truth. Yet it is the rule for me unconsciously to presume that I can safely do violence to any of my living beyond my recognizable range of self-defining sensibility. I now sense every so-called impersonal word as injurious to my vocabulary, as inhibiting my feeling its rightful contribution to my treasuring my primal power, glory, and personal initiative. Every insightless naming of my not-I living is, and must be, clearly my illusional "acting out," my believing I can somehow go or get out of my mind (technically called "transference").

Since I renounce entirely the bare possibility of any communication performance in my language, I close this chapter with an incomplete list of the real functions of my *conscious* wording. It is only naming my living that

1) means only its own self's feeling, a sound of human emotion.
2) refers only to its creator: individual mind.
3) reveals or conceals only self love and its variants, such as its opposites.
4) obliges me to recognize and appreciate my divinity.
5) allows my mind to develop its self helpfulness by growing
   (a) my fellowman verbalizing his emotionality.
   (b) my fellowman living his Dorsey verbalizing his emotionality.
6) serves as the unit of all literary invention and satisfaction.
7) indicates my inviolable individuality by way of necessary unity of language of self.
8) distinctifies each of my definitions by naming it.
9) furnishes the paradigm for the study and use of any of my world.
10) contributes to conscious mentality, to the recognizable living of my self by my self, to my science and religion of my soul (self).
11) provides signs of conscious self experience for augmenting conscious self knowledge and its associated life appreciation.
12) furthers *conscious* self possession and self continence.
13) clears my view of my mental power, as a whole.
14) reveals and records my working of my mind.
15) establishes a base for constructing a greatly needed flexible grammar and rhetoric true to the real nature of my individual mind.

16) supplies a method for exercising mental power, thus preventing its atrophy.
17) serves to distract my attention from self experience which I cannot yet consciously tolerate as being integral to my conscious self love.
18) helps manifest the lifesaving importance of 1) self consciousness and 2) resistance to self consciousness.
19) contributes to my study, understanding and functioning of my *solipsistic* nature.
20) helps to create and dispel helpful illusions, delusions, and life concerns of every description.
21) works in establishing and ordering conscious self control.
22) upholds the mental operation of *conscious* introspection, including the growth and development of conscious self feeling.
23) functions to introduce me to my immense power and to my imperative need to cultivate it carefully.
24) subserves recording, to advance accuracy and accessibility of self orientation.
25) facilitates free association.
26) constitutes poetry and every other kind of self literacy.
27) assists resistance and repression, as either a pejorative or meliorative.
28) expedites establishment of my first science of reality: science of self.
29) achieves *all* that any word ever really can, by naming *all* of its own feeling, in terms of each feeling.
30) provides active discipline of conscious self culture.
31) facilitates imagining.

HOW MY MIND WORKS ITS LANGUAGE

I write only for myself, and I wish to declare once and for all that if I write as though I were addressing readers, that is simply because it is easier for me to write only in that form. It is a form, an empty form—I shall never have readers.

Fyodor Dostoevsky, *Notes From Underground*

It is possible for me to cultivate self respect and any other appreciation for my life precisely to the extent that I can and do use my mind to recognize and hold my one basic truth: *Only I can live in any of my experience.* Equipped with this conscious self realization I can develop and discipline each of my powers so that it may exert itself wisely. Therefore, how to keep use of my vocabulary within the province and on the level of my *conscious* self responsibility, is the principal concern motivating this *Psychology of Language.* Such self-culture orientation cannot be found in any dictionary or encyclopedia, but it is the sure source of ideological strength, emotional continence, and wholesome self love. I estimate the value of this volume highly to the degree that it creates a unity of its subject and its style of presentation. The strength of my impulse to publish my conscious solipsistic psychology necessarily derives only from my wish to help my self through my invention of enjoyably experiencing *my* fellowman's helping his self.

Shakespeare's Hamlet sang it, "Come, give us a taste of your quality; come, a passionate speech." Ideological power, all of it, derives from emotion. All thinking, including logic or reasoning, is verbalized affect. Every kind of feeling (sentiment, mood, or any kind or degree of happy or unhappy emotionality) is a derivative of self love.[1] It follows that any so-called powerful ideology must actually amount to full acknowledgement of the only mental condition possible, that of a constantly self loving individual. This life orientation features not only the necessity for self love but also the desirability that self love be

[1] See my *Psychology of Emotion, passim.*

37

honored with acute consciousness. I now enjoy my mind's fitting its presenting emotion with appropriate words. The consequence of this diligence is keenness of sense for my feeling the range and right of my self responsibility, a working consciousness for the sameness of my mind and my emotionality.

However, the fact is that pure and undiluted *selfishness,* which always reflects merely the necessary truth of individuality, is still considered generally in everyone's formal and informal education to be a dangerous, if not diabolical, mental condition calling for as radical as possible extermination. It is only the rare, conscious self educator who has courageously dared to discover the inviolable wholeness of his being and to preserve his augmenting conscious self possession as his only possible reality.

Ever as a young psychiatrist I was unable to see only my own identity in my patient who was resorting to his mind's early developmental power for his self help. Not only did I consider his sign or symptom of severe mental trouble as unhelpful, but also I even used a descriptive term like autism, narcissism, delusion, hallucination, regression, or repression in a pejorative sense, —thus overlooking my own daily or nightly resorting to the same kind of healthful process for restoring my mental strength, during my sleepy daydreaming or night dreaming. Later, as I found my young medical student or resident similarly resorting to regarding his psychiatric term consistently as a kind of alien name-calling, I helped my self by seeing my identity in him also. Again, the self educator who is fully aware that there can be no other method of education, is most needed but rarely found.

Every other self educator dreads a (conscious) solipsistic mental position as being nothing more or less than what he calls "madness." He must conduct his life on the principle that finding his mind would amount to nothing but losing it. He uses his fear of selfishness to inhibit the development of his conscious self growth and diminish his acknowledgeable appreciation for his life itself. He prefers to be stuck with his *status quo* rather than thunderstruck with enlarged conception of his whole greatness.

The necessary result of attempted depersonalization in the interest of describing "impersonal fact" is actually a devitalizing mental process justly deserving of its name, "bloodless psychology." It is only my lively appreciation for my truth that can make it interesting. Treating any of my experience dispassionately serves only to appear to impart a lifeless unimportance to it. My so-called scientific literature is entirely personal (emotional), constituted as it is only of my own living of it. My scientific finding merits as grand, colorful, and beautiful style as I can summon for describing it. There is aesthetic quality in the plain information provided by a telephone book, transportation schedule, catalogue, or the like.

Research on this subject revealing the educator's unrelieved distress about solipsism, to my mind, provides the saddest record my history has to offer. Conversely, the rare accounts of my fellowman's discovering his divine wholeness is my history's most glorious record of man's astonishing ascension to consciousness for his true estate. Discovering providence in honoring the truth of my own individuality, feeling that my truth is always on the side of whatever I live, provides me with the most helpful kind of theodicy.

To add impetus to my lovable feeling of self certitude I try to use all of my language, written, spoken, or gestured, just for labelling my own self observation. I am my only listener, spectator, or observer of any kind. Apart from my own feeling of my being, I am totally unwitnessed. I satisfy my need for self justification (verification) by the following series of conscious self observations, each one based solidly upon facts of my immediate experience ever accessible for further examination (testing as to validity).[2]

I can find my scientific law no exception to my poetic form, as I practice my self awareness. *Recognizing* my language as being nothing but idiolect unites my poetry and science. My mind can be enlightened by its consciousness only to the extent that my language is recognizably descriptive of my mental

[2] Karl Pearson (*The Grammar of Science*, 1892) and Jules Henri Poincaré (*The Foundations of Science*, 1913) elaborate upon the beauty of scientific concepts.

events. My way of life is directed by my mind's method of working itself. I must discipline my mind carefully to use its language entirely as a naming of its elements, and thereby recognize all of my language as being my conscious idiolect. Otherwise my mind tends to allow its language to do its thinking and feeling for it, in other words, to become its unconscious idiolect. I find my ideal of using words, only for the purpose of developing a practical terminology of my own mind, requires me to assume full responsibility for all of my experience.

The all of my wordage, quite as of my every other effort, consists of my self identity, and my discovery of that truth revealed the supreme merit in self rewarding self discipline to wholehearted sanity. My language of conscious self is my language of sanity, my *acknowledgeable* idiolect. I can imagine getting completely out of my self, however. I can either consciously or unconsciously imagine an externality that is totally foreign to me. Consistently as a child I unconsciously deluded my self that I could observe the world outside of me.

Aristophanes honored his Aeschylus, "Thou who first of the Greeks built towers of lofty language." Although Protagoras first systematized language into the form of grammar, Gorgias developed rhetoric, and Socrates demonstrated great philological interest, ancient Grecian philology went even deeper. The exigencies of the Greek's existence demanded a living language. Need was recognized for word usage that might prove itself adequate for describing the fact that the nature of individual life itself is that of innovation. Thus Socrates regarded the written as the mere phantom of the spoken word. The early Greek distrusted written orders, likening the written code to being doctored by formula (treated by rigid medical prescription). He anticipated Wittgenstein's self observation, "to imagine a language means to imagine a form of life."

My friend protested, "If I add just five words a month to my vocabulary, in a few months my friends will wonder who the heck I think I am." Thus, S. I. Hayakawa once put his language feeling to words:[3]

[3]*Language In Action,* New York: Harcourt Brace and Co., 1939, p. 30.

It has been pointed out that human beings by agreement, can make anything stand for anything. Now, human beings have agreed, in the course of centuries of mutual dependency, to let the various noises that they can produce with their lungs, throats, tongues, teeth and lips systematically stand for specified happenings in their nervous systems. We call that system of agreement *language.*

George Santayana looked into his mind consciously and wrote: "The individual is the only seat and focus of social forces. If society and government are to be justified at all, they must be justified in his eyes and by his instincts."

The illusion that language subserves communication between individuals is based upon the wishful assumption that two or more individuals can learn to use the same language in order to try to understand each other, not only through the exchange of words but of nonverbal tones and gestures. Thus the illusions of getting "together" and going "apart" are supported. To illustrate, the parent and child, teacher and pupil, or psychiatrist and patient are thought to be able to work together only if they use the same language.

From Sigmund Freud's pioneer research on hysteria (1908) developed the concepts of body language, and of language characteristic for each mental condition. His work on dream and affect led to his ideas of dream language and affect language. Throughout his published investigations are to be found unique insights regarding mind's varied use of its linguistic and physiognomic powers. I now record *seeming* repetition.

My need to feel consciously lovable is equated with my wish to live and therefore in my mind-awake I resort to the same ways I use to protect my mind-asleep from excitation that is unpleasing. Again I refer to *dream work,* the wonderful discovery of my Professor Freud.[4] Not merely in my acknowledgeable day dreaming do I follow my wish-fulfilling mental functioning but also during what I ordinarily consider to be my wide-awake living. Only when my mind devotes itself to the

[4] Of this discovery Professor Freud recorded, "Insight such as this falls to one's lot but once in a lifetime." (Preface of third revised English edition, 1931, of his *The Interpretation of Dreams.*)

41

functioning of its self consciousness is it fully awake to itself. However, while claiming to be wide awake without activating my self consciousness, I resort to dream work such as displacement, condensation, regard for representability, symbolization, use of opposites, regression, and even secondary elaboration, in order to change my unconscious feelings and thoughts into the pattern I am accustomed to name waking mentation.

I have demonstrated clearly to my self my use of sensation and perception as forms of illusion and hallucination, when I do not fully recognize the complete subjectivity of those vivid self experiences. My inability to feel my self, and thus locate my self, in all of my functioning of my senses amounts to a form of daydreaming.

My wonder never ceases about the wisdom to be found in biblical lore. To illustrate, "As newborn babes, desire the sincere milk of the word, that ye may grow thereby (1 Peter, 2:2), "If any man offend not in word, the same is a perfect man, and able also to bridle the whole body" (James, 3:2). My sane language planning can base itself upon 1) taking no word for granted but rather examining to see if it contains my self, and 2) fully realizing the powerful self consequence in my wording of my living.

I create my every word out of my self, so that my diction cannot make me objective. I am my only school of writing, basing my every assumption as best I can upon one sentiment of my mind: I am all and only individual. Only my self unconsciousness can account for whatever I do not recognize as my self by name, e.g., object. My being *my* only reality, my only reality test must consist in the specifically distinct sensibility with which I live whatever I wish to test. Self conscious Ralph Waldo Emerson pointed out how each individual soul is its self by virtue of its naming its world in its own idiolect. As that world, Walt Whitman felt this truth, "Objects gross and the unseen soul are one."

Working the illusion of "a common tongue," it is easy to imagine apparent gain (of reaching a so-called vast public), but not so easy to notice real disregard for *unalterable integrity of*

42

individuality. The acknowledged student of his mind can see clearly this necessary definition of his individuality: *intact organic wholeness*. His idiolect is a verbal map of his mind, subjective and incommunicable. Whether or not my scientific research is recognized by me as subjective work, has no significance in making it just that. My asserting it to be objective, my denial of its *subjectivity*, is irrelevant as far as its necessarily being my very own self activity is concerned. Every scientist conducts his research in his own ideal way, the only way possible for him, with or without observing it is only and entirely his ever private life. Henry Margenau, Yale's Eugene Higgins Professor of Physics and Natural Philosophy "after years of meditation" on science in civilization decided, "Materialism was a respectable philosophic view at the end of the nineteenth century; it has now become an anachronism." Individuality consciousness is the mental condition of consciously self continent man. However, Shakespeare's Hamlet refers aptly to that "monster, custom, who all sense doth eat." Usage, rather than self consciousness, ever tempts my mind to ease.

My language, honoring my naming the speculative dignity of my psychology, enters into the development of my essential growth that I call my *social* self. My experience in living my fellowman necessitates my seeing and naming my own vivacious identity in this living, if I would discipline my mind with its whole-making power: self consciousness. In this process, of mobilizing my self love to feel my living in my strange friend or antagonist, I always strengthen my inward self by the feeling of conviction that whatever I live is worthy of my approving recognition from my highest possible source of justice based firmly upon my love of survival. However, wherever my comforting belief is there can always be discovered also its very own hurt (inhibited) self, namely, doubt. Nineteenth-century poet Philip James Bailey sensed this unity in seeming duality:

Who never doubted never half believed,
Where doubt, there truth is—'tis her shadow.

Recognizing with Herodotus and Pindar that custom is well

named the Queen of the World, and that one's opinion is ordinarily dictated by his custom, consequently original students of mind have been unanimous in making conscious *doubt* precede its unconscious belief. In his *Novum Organum* Bacon records this marvelous sense:

> Were there a single man to be found with a firmness sufficient to efface from his mind the theories and notions vulgarly received, and to apply his intellect free and without prevention, the best hopes might be entertained of his success.

Justice Holmes voiced his sentiment, "To have doubted one's first principles is the mark of a civilized man." My belief becomes strong only by my believing difficultly. However it is one thing to doubt willingly from established custom through blindness or malice, and quite another thing to doubt well through prudence and wisdom. Again William Hamilton feels his way sensibly,

> Doubt as a permanent state of mind, would be, in fact, little better than an intellectual death. The mind lives as it believes, —it lives in the affirmation of itself.[5]

As far as I can discover I am made of nothing but action, and my belief (including its doubt) for that truth is activity itself. Pascal (*Thoughts*) felt his motility, "In life we always believe that we are seeking repose, while, in reality, all that we ever seek is agitation." Aristotle stirred his conscious self love as he tenderly observed that a child must first naturally and necessarily *believe* in order that he may awaken to his self truth, learn. Language expresses by dynamic wording the operation denoting the real *one* significance in the apparent "many" illusion. Plato named "intuition of unity" the end of his mind's activity. St. Augustine recognized pain to be the feeling of frustration of unity, and beauty to be the fruition of the feeling of unity.

I find the consciously subjective scientist creating spirited

[5] *Lectures on Metaphysics,* I: 64.

literature suggestive of religious scripture. Such recognition of identity reminds me of John Dewey's wise observation (*Reconstruction in Philosophy*): "The religious spirit will be revived because it will be in harmony with men's unquestioned scientific beliefs and their ordinary day-by-day social activities."

CONSTRUCTING MY CONSCIOUS SELF IDENTITY

No language, but the language of the heart.

Alexander Pope

Whatever is alive, is growing its self only. This self growth is called organic development. All I can be, is the existence I become. All of my doing, is nothing but my being. I do what I am; I am what I do. My every activity is a force of my being, called biological process. My every such vital energy may proceed without great resistance, or it may have to modify itself in varying degree to adapt itself to its necessary ordeal. The science of pathology deals with my constitution's physiological processes of consequential struggling.

My language process undergoes innumerable vicissitudes involving its continuing modification. As far as self respect is concerned, its chief alteration results in *my naming my developing feeling of and for my individuality.* I must ordinarily discipline my mental development in a most specific direction in order to build up my *conscious* appreciation for the allness nature of my individuality, in order to honor my intact wholeness. Hence, adequate measure of the full extent of my man's estate is most rarely achieved. Consequently, the idea of the cheapness of human (individual) life sets up, with all of its train of human (individual) ordeal. I personally depreciate the divinity of my human nature exactly to the extent that I help my self by consciously disowning any of my life experience as being personally my own. My impersonalism is my only possible basis for my atheism, or inhumanity.

The more primitive the mind, the less its conscious self-identity contains its divinity meanings, or any other of its meanings. Development of my conscious love of life varies directly with how much of it I can succeed in seeing as my own personal worth. Thus, I may measure my personal appreciation for my self growth in inverse proportion to my insightless appreciation for its popularity.

47

A life of impersonalism is as close as I can get to living death. In that sense, helping my self by consciously disowning any of my experience, amounts to focal suicide. Conversely, my bravely acknowledging experience I formerly repudiated as not mine, amounts to my personally coming alive. What I unwittingly mean by fear of death must be fear associated with arousing my *living* of the idea of dying. Death itself cannot be a living experience. What I mean by it, may be my wish to terminate living, a wish everyone may vaguely indulge without realizing it clearly.

Whenever I live pain or unhappiness of any kind, I am consciously wishing to stop such precious living, if I cannot recognize its lifesaving importance. The Orphean couplet contains ancient effort to account for man's troubles:

> From thy smile, O Jove, sprang the gods,
> But man was born of thy sorrow.

Certainly, unless I see the biological wisdom in my pain and all unhappiness, I must be tempted to live pessimistically. In his last tragedy, even Sophocles described as the best of all possible benefits, not to be born at all. He expressed the sentiment that once man is born his very best course is to hurry back to where he came from. According to Herodotus, the Thracian welcomed death with salvos of satisfaction, but met birth with lamentations.

Misery in all of its manifestations is often shortsightedly described as immedicable. Immedicable it is, fortunately, for it is itself the constitutional medicine of man. Man's capacity for distress is indispensable, warning him about how his way of using his mind is endangering his existence, and counselling him about how to extend his understanding of his unhappy feelings and thus alter his self's culture wholesomely.

Unless I take the trouble to observe what my every word means, in terms of *my* living the sentiment it names, I must go on living as if my words can do my feeling for me. This mental condition, of allowing my language to appear to subject me to it, may exist without my ever finding it out. It produces signs and symptoms of unhappiness, but I am rarely able to interpret them.

My first self created language of my mind establishes itself without my realizing adequately either that I am creating it by *my* self or that it can name only emotional activity about *my* self. Quite the contrary, mostly I am then realizing my two language illusions. The one deceives me to judge I am receiving my language skill from my teacher. The other deceives me to judge that nearly all of my language refers, not to my emotive meaning for the world of *my* self but rather to emotive meaning in an external world.

By overlooking the fact that I teach my self my language to help me understand my self, my language of my self, I can hide from my conscious mind precious consolation derivable only from my sensing my *whole* being. The remedy for this malady of self disesteem, responsible for all disguised or undisguised suicide or homicide, cannot be my esteem or love or worship for another, for that altruism can be possible only as unconscious self appreciation.

The Oriental predecessor of the ancient Greek represented his god as a phantastic animal, or composite man and animal. Then the human nature loving Greek made his god in his own image. It remains for *self conscious* man to observe that *he is* the only God he can know anything about. I regularly observe: It is divine to be human, and human to overlook it. To be insensitive for any of my living, sets a limit to my ability to take care of my self. I am mindful of my Thoreau's observing, "The laws of the universe are not indifferent *but are forever on the side of the most sensitive.*"

For understanding this fearful but helpful language predicament of mine, that sets up and maintains my self unawareness, I aid my self by a simple and striking illustration. My body can support only limited weight while I am growing it. I do not expect an infant or young child to lift a heavy burden an older child can. I must discipline my mind's body in order to become a weight lifter. Also, by graduated exercises I must go about disciplining my mental activity generally to lift and carry its conscious responsibility for being its self.

49

I difficultly discovered that my individuality was not cradled in family living but that rather all that I called family living was created by and in my own living. I did not live in my house or home, for all that I named house or home had all of its existence in my own being only. My mother did not give birth to me—rather I created in and of my own mind *all* that I named mother, father, sister, brother, neighbor, and so on. Growing the specific mental strength to extend my conscious self love to include my constant self development is always a critical test of my self competence. I was far advanced in such soul calisthenics before I could understand my Plato's lovable self observation: Man is the midwife of his own ego.

I often overwhelmed my mind with consciously insupportable excitation as an infant and child, so that I could not honor my home experience for its life sustaining value. I was incapable of the realization that *whatever* I lived was lifesaving, that my every experience represented my only possible way to stay alive, that any and all of my painful unhappy living constituted my only hold on life whenever it would occur. Much less could I realize that if I could know all of the facts necessitating any unpleasing event, that love of truth (my only reality) would ultimately lead me to value it as a lovably desirable occurrence of my own creating.

As an infant I am unable to assume any conscious responsibility for being my self. My need to live love required my enjoying easily lovable developments only. Even into my third year, in speaking I may refer to my self in the third person. "John does this," or "John has that." My self consciousness is my focusing my attention upon my meaning for my own existence. *This acknowledging responsibility for being my self, is the heaviest kind of mental weight, for I find I must heed carefully and caringly whatever I live with love.* Therefore, extending conscious self love is seldom adopted as a way of life. However, absence of sufficient conscious self identity accounts for the craving for anonymity characteristic of mobster, organization man, dictator, and every other individual who cannot live *his* meaning for his fellowman as an individuation of his own self's meaning. Presence of extended self love accounts for

50

any and all appreciation for human individuality. Humanity is nothing but a word in the mind of the individual employing it, usually unconsciously, to designate all of *his* mankind.

My concept of my self identity enjoys accelerated growth as my increasing locomotion unceremoniously introduces me to one discrete self after another of my world. Especially on account of my professional work, necessitating my identifying my self in extremes of my human individualism, I have disciplined my mind in conscious mental weight lifting. The heaviest weight of all is: *consciously loving responsibility for whatever I experience.* The best inducement to my living my all with love is this *awareness* for my self involvement. All love of adventure is really love of expectant self development. All fear of the future is really fear of expectant self development that cannot be lovingly appreciated.

I see *my* fellowman, each one, as truly wonderful. However, I see each one varying, as I do, in his disciplined power to make his self *conscious* for his wonderfulness. My meliorative term can be used for conscious self repudiation, quite as can my pejorative term. To observe that I am better than I was, is a form of faultfinding too. Thus I can exclude from conscious self identity not only whatever I associate with dislike but also whatever I associate with love or adoration. I may not include either my mate or my maker in my conscious self appreciation.

All dispute is based upon the illusion of plurality, and is traceable to the truth that disputants cannot be talking about the same individual, namely, each one's own self. Furthermore, if they could there naturally would be no dispute. A notable instance in point is the ever continuing illusion of dialogue as to whether or not the term mind is equivalent to the term consciousness. As is true of every problem this one too can be resolved into a phantom problem produced by the insufficient factuality entering into the posing of it.

In my scientific research I help my self most by beginning and continuing with each truth: 1) *consciousness is always a given individual's mind consciousness,* and 2) *acknowledging this essential fact is regularly honored in the breach rather than in the observance.*

From its beginning in my infanthood my every mental activity is my own. My each sensation and perception consists only of my mental activity. Whatever my mind experiences, such as emotion, knowledge, or effort, is entirely its own creation. Only my own self identity can account in any way for whatever my mind lives.

All of my awareness *is* my own. I may be aware for any mental event however without undertaking the specific act of *claiming* it as being entirely and only my own, and this desideratum is characteristic for the way I work my mind during most of its development. I luxuriate in my "embarrassment of riches" my mind provides without a care for responsibly heeding the truth that it is mine, all mine. I merely raise no question about it, until I introduce the necessity for that phantom question when I first start to dissociate my mind into my acknowledgeable and unacknowledgeable I-living. When that happens I suddenly find that I am living my awareness as if it is *not* all mine, as if it is applicable also to my living that I am designating as not-I.

It is precisely at this stage in my psychogenesis that I find I can no longer use my so-called consciousness to apply to all of my mental events exciting my awareness, and that I can and must use my mind also as if it is not consciously mine. Only my feeling of understanding for this train of my mental events can ever get me back upon the track of living all of my consciousness for what it truly is, namely, *my own mind's self feeling.*

It is natural that I comfort my self as a child with the truth that I always did all that I could do and that, therefore, I need not look to my self for understanding the presenting new state of my affairs. I then settled for living some of my being as I and the rest of it as not-I, without any conscious realization of the disastrous consequences of this momentous decision.

However, in order for me to restore my feeling of consciousness for my whole mind as it is ever expressed in any and all of its activity, I must take the trouble of holding my self fully responsible for the way I work my mind and thereby gradually work it through and through as it excites its self's consciousness in all of its living. This work constitutes my process of self analysis that is indispensable for my recognizing my integral being in my every new mental experience.

I honor my choice design for living, of gradually building up the required conscious mental tolerance to call my world my own and my all my world, as my difficult and correspondingly rewarding *scholarly* education of my lovable mind. It is my most self enriching experience to be able to observe, "I *am* all of my world; I can 'have' nothing of an 'external' world." Ancient Aristotle observes, "It is not wealth but character that lasts," and "Man's happiness consists in the free exercise of his highest faculties." My free consecration to consciousness for my personal life is my functioning that subsumes all other sources of self satisfaction.

The point needs to be made. Although the mind of a child just learning to talk is not yet strong enough to work up its special meaning for its self identity, this young and sensitive mind *is* gradually growing its experience it is ultimately to identify as father or mother. Fortunate is the child who can identify as his parent, one who has already developed the conscious mental strength to recognize his own sensation, perception or whatever, as strictly *his* own self experience. For thereby the language-growing child constructs in his own mind a beach-head of responsible self identity. This conscious parental self-starter is of indispensable meaning for the child's difficultly teaching his self how to understand his living of his world as being his "coming to his senses," and "keeping his wits about his self." Chilon asked the Oracle, "What is of all things the best?" Forth came the response, "To know thy self."

Of my living presently, my infinity is local, here. My eternity is momentary, now. "Time" is the illusion of duration comforting me about the eternity of now. "Temporal order" accounts for growth ("change") in personal identity. Expectation is a meaning mitigating timelessness of eternity, as spatial measurement leavens the meaning of infinity. My illusion of motion is analogous to that of time. Successive stills are to motion what successive nows are to time. The *stability* of truth of here and now is always lived by me.

I am consciously humane to the extent that I can be self aware, and only to that extent. What I experience is what I live. My every mental event is self action that exists in its own right, and does not collapse into the nothingness of otherness. Quite as my Kant conceived it for his self, so I observe that whatever I will, feel, think, or otherwise mind, is a creation of my own life's growing.

My understanding is all and only about itself. Whenever I loosely observe that I understand something, all I really mean by it (or can mean by it) is that I sense my own lovable identity in the living of what I claim to understand. My sense of personal identity, my independent self awareness, is present whereever I possess understanding. It is self comforting to limit my understanding to what is easy to understand and to turn from all else with my complaint, "That is too difficult to understand," or even, "That is not understandable." Obviously I make no provision for my extending my capacity for understanding by such soft living.

My neglecting to distinguish only my self in my every word is costly self disregard which permits me to avoid exertion of self care in behalf of seemingly undesirable elements of my self from which I have therefore withheld my interest. To give to any word the meaning of reality without recognizing my self as the only subsistence of that reality is to try to hypostatize that word at the expense of conscious hypostatization of my self.

Any and every so-called misunderstanding or disagreement is symptomatic of specific linguistic difficulties created by the illusion "a common tongue," and curable by specific linguistic healing power deriving from recognizing all possible language as an idiolect. Thus one's most glorious attribute is his insight for his sacred language of self, enabling his feeling his own genius in his diction. What passes for dialogue or conversation or communication is best revealed as a mixture of acknowledged and unacknowledged individuality in each so-called participant. All human understanding is nothing but acknowledgeable personal identity. One's words can be drawn only from the breath of his own human life, from the birth pangs of his own linguistic conceptions. Seeing one's words from this high van-

54

tage ground composes the sane speech and the eloquence which one's fellowman loves most to acknowledge and originate responsibly as his own.

For the purpose of achieving self sanity it is not at all sufficient to quote Pope's brilliant, "The proper study of mankind is man." The proper study of mankind can be found only as: individual man's study of his individual self. For this study every person needs urgently a special kind of vocabulary which provides him with names for consciously labeling his own self's elements only. This is the great line of speculation which the semanticist finds most rewarding whenever he is ready to work it. There is and can be no use of language which is not that of a given individual, and every acknowledged great one of all time, beginning with Jehovah's I AM, has recognized his speaking, writing, and reading are, and must be, only autobiographical. Despite his innumerable aliases (self misnomers) everyone's matchless, singular life runs a course wholly and entirely of its own. Sensing only one's self in one's word, phrase, sentence, or theme, goes to the very height of one's subject, not beyond it. If I impose restriction upon my imagination of my greatness I shall see many signs of my apparently trifling littleness. Appeal to self observation, strongest of all possible calls to humanity's defense, is impossible except in the speaker who can observe that only he can hear or answer his appeal.

I choose my conscious poet as my ideal linguist. What makes his words sing is their expression of the rate, rhythm, impetus, and passionate sensibility of his human nature. His immediate living sounds in them. Other oratory, the result of dispassionate quest for verbal perfection, is wanting in this spirit of immediate self vivacity, and proves contrived. A poet does not master his poem, but sees his own exuberant self spontaneity tonic in it. He does not look at his poetry "objectively," but rather senses his subjectivity dictated in its words. His words are hot-breathed self concentrations, not seeming self diversions. His style of composition superbly illustrates what its content exalts for due enjoyment: mind imaginatively confronting its fathoming oneness, wholeness, powerfulness, nowness, hereness, allness. His poem is his theory of poetry.

Uniquely the poet integrates his being and minding so that the emotive meaning of his words manifests the real presence of his living. He writes his self down spiritedly, confidingly, uninhibitedly. His pen is swift, impetuous, gushing, realizing actual life in words, restoring the primal unity of linguistic sense and meaning. His language seems to emote mind itself, not merely name it. It is thus self realized mysticism which each lover of life (unfrightened by his own native greatness) finds in his poet, takes to heart and cherishes as valuable personal identity, trustworthy reality, mental independence.

It is lifesaving to know the significance of conscious self observation, as of conscious self disregard. René Fülöp-Miller notices,[1] "More and more, from the language used in the mechanized century, words which could arouse an image of the organically complete human being tended to go out of use." He describes how the Bolshevik "theoreticians of art" repudiated individual endowment. "For them, imaginative writing was nothing more than 'verbal chemistry' which could be turned out in laboratories under the guidance of experienced 'word chemists' in accordance with suitable formulae and recipes."

My every word that distracts me from my own being is a drain on my life appreciation, a foreign body in the corpus of my conscious self knowledge. I make my own my John Morley's linguistic ideal, a "steadfast use of a language in which truth can be told; a speech that is strong by natural force." To this end I originate my John Franklin Genung's definition of rhetoric (*The Working Principles of Rhetoric,* 1900): "the art of adapting discourse, in a harmony with its subject and occasion, to the requirements of a reader or hearer."

Whenever I cannot recognize a feeling as being exactly as it ought to be, it is thereby already undergoing repression. All literacy is self literacy, entirely personal. For me, being impersonal in my language is being illiterate. Conscious self wording is my language of sanity. Surely this new look at my self has often seemed disconcerting rather than consoling, but my

[1] *Leaders, Dreamers and Rebels,* trans. Eden and Cedar Paul, New York: Viking Press, 1935, p. 352, 356, and 357.

dependence upon my truth requires me to be at all times ready to add to my understanding, whenever my further self experience justifies it. I well recall my Professor Freud's helpful self observation during my self analysis: "Unconscious, —that is only a word."

This book's wordage sets up as an authority merely for its author, and only as far as its statements, rigorously tested, have proved self justifying. Everyone considers that he knows what his language is. And everyone is right according to his lights. Furthermore, only I can know anything at all about my language. Experience teaches me that the neglect of this one linguistic fact is most common and most costly. For example, only respect for its basic truth can force me heedfully to find, rather than heedlessly to overlook, my mind in my work.

It helps me to be specially sensitive to the ease with which *naming* leads to classifying, and therefore to regard my self as constituting my only class. Appreciating being in a class by my self enables me to attribute identical complexibility to my fellow existent. When my words do not clearly designate selfness, I imply that I can objectify or personify. The ancient Greek philosopher prized his *logos* as most meaningful, as signifying both word and "measure." As Protagoras claimed, "Man is the measure of all things." Anaximander held, "The sun will not overstep his measures, if he does the Erinyes, the handmaids of justice, will find him out." Only my appreciation that my every speech meaning (feeling) is all and only about my very own self (my world) enables me to see that my whole life is always and entirely about my own marvelous human being. My denying the right to be of this or of any other persuasion has no other consequence than my ignoring some of my very own personal identity.

A linguist's life is made steadily proportionate to his true greatness once he chooses the difficult course of discipline in self consciousness. In growing awareness for his self continence he must arduously extend the bounds of his conscious self tolerance (self love). In his lax everyday word-art, as well as sensory and perceptual language, he finds he is lamentably illiterate (impersonal) and correspondingly unnatural as far as his natural literary style is concerned, since it has long since cramped itself with rigid rules of grammar and logic. His devotion to his grammatical apparatus has served to distract him from enjoying his wonderful experimentation of consciously living his self world. Linguistically sophisticated is rarely the same as word wise.

Consciously word-oriented Alfred Korzybski predicted, "A new school of history will arise which will show to mankind what disasters the wrong conception of man by man has wrought to mankind." For achieving, preserving, and restoring my conscious mental balance, I have found it necessary to view my language as entirely and only my self designating musical and poetic power enabling me to cultivate and refine my aesthetic appreciation for my ongoing subjectivity. Such discipline in self responsibility has cultivated holistic and personalistic appreciation in my life orientation, each ministering to my conscious self analysis. Thus I translate the seemingly impersonal discoveries of aesthetics and epistemology into discoveries of my own real personal growth. Therefore I do not have to deny my life affirming self satisfaction to my scientific exactness of any kind, e.g., chemical or mathematical formula. Whatever is true is also beautiful.

MY UNITED SELF

The higher education so much needed today is not given in the school, is not to be bought in the market place, but it has to be wrought out in each one of us for himself.

William Osler, M.D.

Ernst Cassirer observes that in his language man can do no more than to build up his own universe. He points out that the wisdom in appreciating the allness of the wholeness of individual man has been known to be available to one ready to make use of it ever since Parmenides (515-440 B. C.). Irving J. Lee responsibly asserted,[1] "If in our talk we split what is not to be found so split in nature, our talk is better classified as fiction and fancy." I can awaken only to my self, whether I acknowledge that fact or not. My sensing of my very own personal identity underlying all seeming "difference" or non-identity provides an enormous economy of effort. Observed single-minded Aristotle, Knowledge of opposites is one.

I cannot "have" a sensation or perception or thought, or understanding, or feeling, —I *am* it, and must *be* it. The word "having" is divisive, the word "being" is unitive, in tendency. Which auxiliary verb I use therefore decides whether I shall seem to my self to be living self affirmingly or self negatingly. To *be* somewhere else, or to *be* whatever, *I* must be it. To know consciously I must be sensing my identity. I strive for emotionality in my scientific writing, emotionality of the specific kind that illustrates clearly its author's conscious control of it as he lets loose its intrinsic power in word and phrase.

I trace powerful writing to powerful author. As I live with consciousness for my wholeness and allness so can my writing style contain that quality of integrity. If I wish my literary effort to be characterized by any special virtue, I can attain my wish by disciplining my whole self to be of that virtue. This

[1] *Language Habits in Human Affairs,* New York: Harper and Brothers, 1941.

Psychology of Language must illustrate my present conscious design for conducting my life, namely, my enjoying my controlled emotionality.

How strongly I will to understand my self, to feel my intelligibility, must come out in the clarity of my writing, in my fidelity to my denotation and connotation of autonomy in my word, phrase, or sentence. Thus I aim at precision in meaning definitely and literally what I say or write in, to, and for my self. Attaining such precision depends mainly upon my exciting my self consciousness while I am writing or speaking. It is noteworthy that this method is just the opposite of my popular one of trying to forget my self as I speak in order to avoid "buck fever" or "stage fright." However I have discovered such embarrassment is not due to the presence of too much self consciousness, but rather to the insufficiency of it that prevents my sensing everyone of my audience as my own creation, subject to me, not I to "it."

The specific unity of linguistics and linguist is inviolable. This fact that language has its only existence and relevance in the individual living (creating) it, is worthy of most heedful consideration. Therefore my wish to adapt my style to the comprehension of my reader is practicable only according to my reader's readiness to cope with the intrinsic difficulty inherent in consciously solipsistic writing. Developing kind feeling for acknowledgeable idiolect depends upon the individual reader's own devotion to it, rather than upon the perspicuity in his author's defining it. The truth that all language is only the verbalization of the linguist's emotion is not easily seen thoroughly. Despite any of my splendor of diction, or lack of it, I can put to word only the emotive truth of my incommunicable and unbridgeable individuality.

My passion for self consciousness must assert itself as my ruling passion. My backbone must be the recognizable backbone of my composition. When my enthusiasm for my wholeness and allness kindles the deep emotion of my being my world of self it must infuse all of the vigorous force of living into my style that I can summon. I persistently present my conscious self orientation, thoroughly enjoying the opportunity for this

60

fact to speak for itself emphatically, over and over. It is my intention to transcribe my *sensing* the importance of my disciplining my living with self consciousness. Greatest linguistic liability for me is that any word develop the significance of being "objective" rather than *subjective,* and static rather than dynamic.

Wilhelm von Humboldt offers this genetic, dynamic definition of wording: the ever exerted effort of the spirit to make the articulated sound able to express thinking, and provide "a real world, which the spirit must set between itself and objects by an inner exertion of its powers," wherewith "the soul is on its way to finding more and more in language and to putting more and more into it."

Thus I note my linguist's appreciation for the psychic, the meaningful emotion of meaning. Novalis specifies, "Spirit is self-contained being."Sir Arthur Eddington identifies reality as spirit and consciousness. But however one wishes to name his creating self (idealizing, subjectivizing, inspiriting, animating, feeling, or whatever), the one all-important understanding for my study is that such a name-place is always strictly and wholly one's very own. Yet it is self potentiating to renounce the apparent fixation value of naming, to recognize its lifelike mobility. Reverence for the spiritual quality of language reflects ideal literary deportment. The word's living activity favors rather than obstructs its function of signification. *The joy of living underlies every joy.*

Accuracy of definition underlies purity of diction. Habitually used wording serves worthy purpose as does neologistic liberty. All of my stressing the incommunicable nature of language, its being absolutely each linguist's idolect naming only the elements of his strictly personal mind, is essential for my everyone's honoring adequately, in terms of his own living, all that he can mean by his fellowman or by any of his living of his world, as well as all that he can mean by his linguistic heritage from his illustrious ancestors.

Whatever is, consists of its creating itself, exists only in its makings. The reality in every noun is this verbal being which composes it. On every level of my being, my sensation is constituted only of my sensing my self. I must see to it persever-ingly and painstakingly that my very own sensing, perceiving, or experiencing of any kind, does not appear to be able to dis-engage from me, become objective rather than *subjective,* and seem to react upon me as if an extrinsic, alien existence.

My wishing is my ever present reality that inconspicuously contributes to such appearing or seeming of impersonal "other-ness." Whatever I cannot recognize is already my own living may be wished for as if it is not already being lived by me. As a child I already lived *my* parent's greatness but could not recog-nize that truth except in the form of my wish to become great like my parent. For me all that can constitute truth, or beauty, or goodness, or any interesting living whatever, consists in the process of its making itself with my productive imagination. All that makes up my thought is my process of thinking. Any so-called fact is its actuality, unifying emotional element, in its self-realizing activity. Goethe apperceptively describes fact as consisting of theory.

How easily my word can appear to confound me! Living, duration of being, is self activity, one's only experience of so-called space, time, or motion. Whatever exists, consists of itself only, and only the way it exists can distinctify it. Only present, now and here, can exist. St. Augustine's dictum holds: there are not three temporal orders (past, present, and future) but only one (*present*). Number is an illusion analogous to motion, created by inattention to the oneness of the percept (or con-cept) "manifold." There can be no stamp of collectivity on individuality. I am consciously a one passion man, a one idea man, that is, a one *man* man.

A word can speak only for itself. Mind conscious Cassirer (1957) observed and recorded that the Greek language desig-nates thought and speech by the same term. My language consciousness is needed to picture, not efface, my only ground of all knowing: my feeling of self consciousness, the only source of my psychology of sanity. I can discipline my emo-tionality to be able to feel self conscious even while its excite-ment runs high. Shakespeare makes his Hamlet create this truth in his advising the players: "use all gently: for in the very torrent, tempest, and, as I may say, whirlwind of your passion, you must acquire and beget a temperance that may give it smoothness" (Act III, Scene 2).

My every word not only names but constitutes spontaneous vivid selfness of mine, and my sensing that realization helpfully enters into my choice of words. A trope such as a metonym or a metaphor, a personification or a plural, indeed any needed attention to grammatical form, may obscure my sense of my constantly growing personal identity in it and thus offer the appearance of speech based upon impossible operations. Alexander Gode's wise discernment finds that language not only presents a verbal map of self experience but also creates a verbal model of whatever it names.

Hence it is that every self conscious psychologist is willing to study his use of words enough to understand all of it as literally growing his self appreciation. For example, Sigmund Freud's interest in his language was profound and sustained. Hughlings Jackson, Henry Head, Adhèmar Gelb, Kurt Goldstein, Samuel T. Orton, Lee Edward Travis, George V. Bohman and many others have traced complicated linguistic formations to modifications in the linguist's organicity. Einstein built up an entirely new vocabulary for naming his daring cognition. Cassirer recognized that every word in his thoughtful sentences is sensed, that naming is no exception to meaning. Conscious individualist Montaigne felt, "He who would fight custom with grammar is a fool."

Richard Grant White (1821–1885), American Shakespearean scholar, passionately asserted, "There is a misuse of words which can be justified by no authority, however great, by no usage, however general." R. G. Latham (1812–1888) renowned English linguist decided, in language "whatever is, is right." A literary error was once called to the attention of Walt Whitman. He replied he preferred to let it be, for he must have meant something by it! Quite as might be expected, my review of literature indicates that the conscious individualist tries to free his language so that he can further free his self with it.

I consider my language to be well made only as far as it painstakingly localizes all of my world in my individuality. My repeating this literary requirement in various terms brings to view new aspects of its deeply satisfying recognition of my living of all of my universe. My enforcement of my consciousness for my living whatever I live builds up my life's worth so that I can gradually proceed at last in climactically appreciating my only real possibility for appreciation: my whole inviolable allness, my absolute owndom, my illimitable united Self. Beyond doubt my most valuable way to choose an accurate and vital word is provided by my intimate feeling of my subjective (ideal, spiritual) involvement in it in the sense that it derives from my creativity. It is most difficult of all to cultivate a vocabulary which implies nothing but self consciousness, but self reference wording is the only reliable peaceful one. Many and mighty are the linguistic obstructions to self consciousness. Nevertheless, since I regard my only real success to be that of staying alive, of being the continuant of my living individuality, it behooves me to make the most of my awareness for my self. *My indispensable success consists of my self's succeeding its self.* To achieve purity of my language therefore I must aim at keeping unsullied my self-tongue rather than merely my mother-tongue.

Difficult as it may be to find the uniquely specific word for any of my scientific writing, it is also difficultly desirable to employ only a term that I can appreciate as a name for my own living. All of my science must be nothing but a science of my self although it may never, or hardly ever, be *conscious* science of my self. Before becoming sensitive for this truth I tended to oppose my every other science with my vainly desired science of self. I enjoyed a happy conscious integration when I could *feel* all of my scientific living as my purely personal living. Present policy in my scientific literature is its editor's insisting upon his author's reportorial usage of dictatorial "we," rather than self honoring "I." Such a policy does not favor either the editor's or the author's developing desirable conscious integration of his scientific work and his conscious living. Repetitious? then, so is my breathing.

Apt usage of the following questions pursues my most important self observation:

1) How do my words contribute to my individual scientific

research upon my human nature?

2) How do my words contribute to my distracting my self from recognizing my one and only source of sane knowledge, namely, my conscious self development?

My living is a constant putting on of the new man, a constant creating of my novel self, but my manneristic, stereotyped language provides me with the illusion of maintaining a conservative permanent structure which only my cultivation of my word consciousness can expose (and hence dispel). It appears that in everyone's language trouble, a creature of habit supplants a creature of self insight. My conscious emotional continence, my only foundation for self insight, relieves my mind of its verbal *addictions*. "A true 'living language' would have a fresh denotion for the singularity of every mental creation, for every view of the ever flowing mind."[2] Horace claimed "Fashion . . . sole umpire, arbitress, and guide of speech," adding:

> Full many a word now lost—again shall rise,
> And many a word shall droop which now we prize.

In *The Poet,* Emerson says, "The etymologist finds the deadest word to have been once a brilliant picture." Thus an eminent author, expecially distinguished in word study, strives to free his idiolect, but a self unconscious pedant, purist, or minor grammarian will seek to bind what he calls "the common tongue." Thomas Jefferson would justly consider usage "as giving law to grammar, and not grammar to usage."

Mental health is conscious wholeness,—not the absence of so-called insane tendencies, but the functioning "balance of a thousand insanities" (Emerson). Hence the vitalizing value of acknowledging personal responsibility for my words. It is the privilege of the free soul to enjoy knowing its self.

By "word consciousness" I mean specifically: Word self consciousness, that is, the necessity that my verbalism be

---

[2] Cf. Leo Spitzer, *Linguistics and Literary History, Essays in Stylistics,* Princeton: Princeton University Press, 1948.

understood as all and only a wording for my subjectivity. Language appears to misprize its user in any word which does not *noticeably* prize him. If I work hard enough at it, my linguistics can clearly verbalize me as all in one piece, define me somewhat (in Carlton Laird's phrase), "as united in Holy Wordlock." C. K. Ogden and I. A. Richards would give to every word its due, considering that the central subject subsuming grammar, rhetoric, philology, phonetics, semantics—each of the linguistic fields—might well be termed Orthology. Said Jean Paul, "Children could never learn to speak if they did not already possess language." Said Wilhelm von Humboldt, "Language must, in accordance with my deepest conviction, be considered part of the very constitution of man." Said Jacob Grimm, "Thinking is speaking to oneself; every thinking person is both first and second person."

Speaking or writing is feeling and thinking for one's self, of one's self. My use of wording other than that of naming my self feeling courts the whirlwind's dismissal (as of Elihu):

> Who is this, darkening counsel
> With words, —but without knowledge?

The use of my language for technically furthering my *conscious* self culture frees me from any appearance of unconscious display. There is a pointedness of truth in every word I can *feel* my self in. It makes the poetry of my life. *Living* language grows as the very tissue of my spirit, —no seemingly chance growth, or foreign addition in me. Giving my every experience a name that I can acknowledge as a synonym for my own is a process of consciously naturalizing my diction. I never can feel strange or affected as long as I feel the conviction and power of self consciousness. I, only I, am always here and now, —all else must be my anachorism and anachronism.

Nevertheless as I put out my tongue, in the sense of heeding its accuracy, I cannot but notice my innumerable linguistic "expressions of a convenient dimness, under which inexact thinkers often hide an abundance of indefinite or erroneous conceptions."[3] My every pejorative word is a sign of ignored goodness. I find Algernon Charles Swinburne enjoying his literary complaint:

> The wildest, the roughest, the crudest offspring of literary impulse working blindly on the passionate elements of excitable ingorance was never more formless, more incoherent, more defective in the structure, than this voluminous abortion of deliberate intelligence and conscientious culture.

Knowing that pejoration merely expresses an "ouch" for a nursed hurt of mine, thereby indicating a present limit of my *recognizable* self tolerance only, I make it my intention to treat each of my pejoratives understandingly so that I can use it without seeming to be used by it.

Just as a new invention can develop its entirely new vocabulary, so discovery of new aspects of emotionality may require additional diction. Indeed, once the reality of solipsism takes hold the courage to attempt a new poetry of it is sure to produce itself. Certainly there can be no stronger appeal to linguistic genius than that of a *conscious* language of self. Right now I thrill to the sound and scene of my rare literary artist who *sings* his language consciously as serving only his very own life's purpose and pleasure. Of this uniquely charming conception of his diction is my Jehovah or Job, quite as is my Shakespeare, Emerson, Thoreau, or Whitman.

Indeed, insightless association of any feeling of unpleasantness with anything besides the unpleasantness itself, is the origin of repression (self repudiation). I know of no greater wisdom of living than that of increasing my capacity to love consciously whatever I live, for after all it is only my own personal living I am ever experiencing (living). Love is the feeling natural to living and every other feeling is a modification of love, rarely recognizable as love.

To illustrate, hate is hurt love, fear is threatened love, guilt is repudiated love, shame is embarrassed love, jealousy is dislo-

[3] William Dwight Whitney, *The Life and Growth of Language—An Outline of Linguistic Science,* New York: D. Appleton and Co., 1876.

67

cated love, and so on. Going from love to anger or humiliation or whatever feeling, just appears to be changing my lifelong subject of love. Every kind of pain or unhappiness is love protecting itself. Regardless of contrary appearance reenforced by semantic habit implying unselfishness, (my) everyone *always* does as he pleases and *always* conducts his life (however short-sightedly) self helpfully.[4]

As an educator my interest in advancing learning extends largely to miscalled impersonal knowledge, but my interest in extending my knowledge of my emotionally charged capacities is also now aroused. By studying the biological adequacy of *all* of my emotionality I systematically discover a rugged but polishable self potential beneath the overlay of my erudite sociality. Unquestionably it is hard to get at emotionality for purpose of studying it for that technique must depend entirely upon the degree to which the investigator has arduously worked up his own conscious emotional continence.

Whatever is, is all and only about itself, and is its own everything. Only its nothing exists outside of anything, or anyone. Every particular consists entirely of its universality. Whatever is, is incommunicable. Speech is always only a form of its speaker's growing aloud. Love power clearly unites life's all, by turning unhappy self rejection into peaceful vitality, by reducing all apparent foreignness to the real personal identity which it is. Selecting language for its qualities of sound features this identity (euphony, onomatopoesis). Self reverence is the life orientation providing "the Divine look" that sees all as perfect. My idiom of mind reveals what awareness I have for my wonderfulness, for my thorough excellence.

Observantly in his helpful *English Prose* (1890), John Earle (1824–1903) personifies grammar as being the natural enemy of idiom, as continually trying to popularize (subjugate) its individualism with conventional rule. Even my dictionary reflects a kind of literary morality so that I may not be able to find in it exciting but unmentionable wording for most intimately personal living considered to be unsavory, coarse,

---

[4] *Psychology of Emotion, passim.*

68

vulgar, or obscene. *The American Heritage Dictionary of the English Language*[5] now at last respects numerous "unspeakable" terms, including most of the "infamous four-letter words."

Despite my feeling constant linguistic pressure to "popularize" my vocabulary, to respectabilize it, I find it possible to awaken consciousness for my individuality merely by increasingly frequent usage of the word "my." I frequently quote my highly esteemed James Harvey Robinson:

> The little word *my* is the most important one in all human affairs, and properly to reckon with it is the beginning of wisdom. It has the same force whether it is my dinner, my dog, and my house, or my faith, my country, and my "God."

The reality of every idea of nominalism, or the naming of every idea of realism, always proves to be in the mind of its realizer. My language can never designate whatever I am not. No word of mine can ever be (exist) independent of my living it. The serious trouble is that every word of mine can exist without my consciousness that it is mine. Often I neglect clothing my meaning in the language "of real life" (Wordsworth), so that it does not appear to be humanized (that is, individualized). Thus, I easily overlook my personal identity in my education's vocabulary, unless I make a point of feeling (heeding) it. I must make my language for my self, if I would avoid the appearance of making my self for language.

Wording is living, and the wording of my childhood resembles my current wording, quite as all of my current looks have taken on modification of my developing emotionality. Professor Earle reported, 1890, of new terms: "The coining industry in the present age of English Prose will be found to draw its materials mainly from the vernacular, and far less than formerly from classical sources."

Although I may not recognize my self in my word, nevertheless I use personification very frequently as a language device

[5] Boston and New York: American Heritage Publishing Co., Inc. and Houghton Mifflin Co., 1969.

to make so-called impersonal perception, abstraction, and naming personally acceptable. James Russell Lowell described the use of capital letters to name mental or moral attributes as "that alphabetic personification which enlivens all such words as Hunger, Solitude, Freedom, by the easy magic of an initial capital."

As long as I can delude my self that someone else can speak to me I shall not have to face the importance of my need to speak precisely to my self. As long as I can delude my self that someone else can do my listening for me, I shall not have to face my responsibility for listening to what I say. My most popular educational fallacy, communication, obstructs my view of my mental integration. One cannot speak to, or be spoken to by, another. What I may consider to be "hearing my fellow-man speak to me," is always nothing but my growing of my own audile experience of (my) his speaking and listening to his self, which I may mistake for communication. The comforting illusion of not being absolutely alone derives strongest verbal support from the implication of social intercourse served by such a term as communication, conversation, or dialogue. In his speech, "A Literary Enthusiasm; or, The User Used" Roy P. Basler good naturedly observes:[6]

> College students today seem to have waked up to the fact that they are being used to perpetuate an intellectual community and a socioeconomic establishment that has its own selfish interest at heart more than theirs. Whatever their individual variety of revolt— new left, black militant, or drug-oriented flower children—they all agree that they won't be used by an establishment which seems to them hypocritical, not to say dishonest, in its use of human beings in general, and of young people in particular.

The truth needs exercise, one can never in any way experience anyone or anything but his own inviolable self. I often remind my self of this insight of John Keats: "We read fine things but we really do not understand them until we have gone the same steps as the author." Cassirer observed of his self, I cannot

---

[6] Phi Beta Kappa Address, College of William and Mary, December 5, 1969.

turn my back upon my own linguistic self for it too is my own basic spiritual force:

Shakespeare, aptly named by Lytton Strachey "by far the greatest word-master who ever lived," is correspondingly one of the greatest psychologists. He uses the power of words justly, that is, to provide utmost range for the freedom of his imagination. He did not hesitate to call into question that power in his word-picture of impassioned Juliet asking Romeo, "What's in a name? . . . doff thy name; And for the name, which is no part of thee, Take all myself." Whatever I quote is strictly intended to verbalize my own original thought.

The word "lie" or "pretence" posits nonexistence, since whatever is, really is. Study of deception always reveals truth underlying its apparent falseness. Every word signifying unworthiness is a pejorative term intended to belittle ever-present greatness of perfection. In this sense, hell is clearly a pejorative. Similarly every meliorative signifies betterment or perfectibility (e.g., improvement) thus implying faultfinding rather than sufficient fact-finding in preceding living. In this sense, heaven is clearly a meliorative. The extent to which I make my language hypostatize something out of nothing or imagine nothing out of something is far too great for me to sense earnestly.

From catching my self in the act of practicing this word magic, I am gradually awakening to my strong need to indulge it. It helps me to spare my self overwhelming unpleasantness associated with acknowledging that I *am* my dislikes just as I *am* my likes, and that my unhappy experience is quite as lifeworthy as my happy one.[7]

Without this feelingful self understanding I must continue to practice my good-bad screening of my literature, *unconsciously finding fault* in such pejorative terms as cant, trite, redundant, affected, worn, over-worked, copied, vulgar, slang. With conscious emotional continence my aim towards literature that pleases me with its author's ideal poesy, continues to be natural and legitimate. However my feeling about my author's

---

[7] *Psychology of Emotion, passim.*

71

writing that does not please me also becomes tempered, moderate, and appreciative for whatever it is able to be.

What my word appears literally to say may not include all that is really in it. I may appear to talk or write on a theme entirely aside from the connotation of my subjectivity, and in such a way that I seem to "lose my self" in my theme. This style serves as communication, as conveying my "impersonal knowledge" to my fellowman, thus enlivening my illusion of objectivity. It is also possible for me to word my scientific or unscientific theme in such a way that my authorship is not only implied but also vivified as illustrated by it. This is my nature underlying my *figurative* language containing the acknowledgeable power of my personality, namely, my emotional self. The test and worth of this consciously autobiographic style is its naturalness, providing the conscious pleasantness of living. The greater this conscious naturalness the greater its author's appreciation for his literary power.[8]

Socrates has Cratylus claim a name is not just a piece of one's voice "applied to the thing . . . there is a kind of inherent correctness in names." *I know of no accurate way of knowing what I am ever meaning by a word except by free associating to it, that is, by using the given word to see what self interest I find my self currently making out of it.* Free association is immediate verbal self recognition.

I find all of my appreciation for "Man" or "Humanity" meaningless to the extent that I try to distinguish it from my realization of my very own self. My study of "the" history of "the" world must be for me a history-of-my-self study. The seeming mere aggregation of factual impersonal knowledge (an impossibility) is really always a (recognized or unrecognized) creation of possible self knowledge articulating with previous conscious self growing and justly deepening self appreciation.

Much of my conscious life has been spent subject to my idea

[8] See Walter H. Seegers, *My Individual Science,* Detroit: Center for Health Education, 1968.

that "the world" I always unconsciously "imagine" is ever so great; that my *individuality,* which is all I can ever really imagine, is comparatively ever so small. Led by that biologically inadequate self-estimate idea, I found it natural to assume that any truly great achievement or advancement of my world issued from events ever foreign to me, from impersonal happenings inexplicably arising from innumerable influences abroad in "the universe." Terms such as culture, civilization, education, evolution, science, nature, divinity, held little or no conscious personal significance for me, —without my noticing that my disowning them must leave them entirely groundless and my acknowledgeable self entirely irresponsible.

My conscious idiolect is ever my only realistic claim to an esperanto. Whenever I realize that my verbalization can refer only to my self, I sense the kind of linguistic sincerity that makes one's word as good as his bond. As I notice this sincere appreciation for my comprehensive individuality, I renew my James Truslow Adams's art of living: "The road of conformity is merely the road back to savagery." I see how my so-called common language must helpfully create the frightening but unrecognizable illusion of the "lost individual."

I see ideally and practically all that constitutes mental trouble, including troubled mind complicating its own body's tribulations, as a rarely understood but vital allegory exposing the living cost of inhibited self love consequent upon unacknowledgeable self unconsciousness.

Reviewing my grammatical figures I observe how each one depends for its being upon emotionality discoverable in the nuclear body scale of my mind. Whatever grammatical figure I use is a label for a specific mood in me, e.g., exclamation, interrogation, hyperbole, irony. Especially apostrophe serves my sensing my intact wholeness by realizing all of my "past" self as present. As Emily Dickinson felt it: "For the faithful, absence is condensed presence." This "historical present" is indispensable for my conscious appreciation of my total unity.

My every word that appears to be a name for not-self proves itself a perfect trope for denoting some rejected aspect of my own living. *Without self even not-self must remain meaningless.* Synecdoche illustrates how each element of me as a subject is an individuation of me. Metonymy (change of name) shows how a single aspect of my wholeness involves all of me. On and on I excite my wonder about my truly marvelous nature as I translate each of my seemingly foreign words into my real *self* naming that it is, and must be. How clearly Shakespeare's Hamlet exclaims conscious self love:

> What a piece of work is man! how noble in reason! how infinite in faculty! in form and moving how express and admirable! in action how like an angel! in apprehension how like a god!

I wish to word the nature of my literary power, its necessarily diffused use for my understanding my experience, its constant reference to its only creator, its indispensable contribution to my life appreciation. In his *Grammar of the English Language* (1818), William Cobbett (1762–1835) declares:[9]

> The word *it* is the greatest trouble that I know of in language. It is so small and so convenient, that few are careful enough in using it. . . . Never put an *it* upon paper without thinking well of what you are about. When I see many *its* in a page, I always tremble for the author.

I sketch the absolutely idiosyncratic nature of every aspect of my word and collocation of words. Any word of mine is not intended to take the place of any word of my reader. His author's sentences may offer helpful portrayal "in addition to," and not "instead of," any of his present linguistic or psychological orientation.

The completely incommunicable nature of all word meaning is rarely recognized. I like to listen to my fellowman speak, in order to hear how he works his mind. His style seems to illus-

---

[9] Pseudonym, Peter Porcupine. Cobbett spent two years (1810–1812) in prison and was fined 1,000 pounds for his article against flogging in the army.

trate his use of his imagination. Only that is clearly recognized that is observed with love. Hence the Augustinian love making: *Non intratur in veritatem nisi per charitatem.* Instead of being some kind of reality to be investigated by objectively valid methods, my every human individual is the suspensive foundation of all that goes by his name of reality.

My chapter "Perspective" records a most consequential distinction particularly worthy of the most careful and caring consideration of every linguist: *any-kind-of-existence is not at all the same as awareness-for-any-kind-of-existence.* This feeling for consciousness merits a prominence according to its tremendous importance. To illustrate, a person is always behaving himself perfectly ideally and desirably, with or without his awareness for the truth that he is always doing (being) all that is currently possible for him. Whatever is, is always in its make-up perfectly, ideally, and desirably just. I treat this truth with cautious reverence for without this factuality to depend upon any scientist must feel helpless indeed. Viscount Falkland's keen mindedness states this force-of-truth sentiment practically, "When it is not necessary to change, it is necessary not to change."

I am being whatever I am doing, whether my action is conscious (voluntary) or unconscious (involuntary) self gesture. Furthermore, I reveal my self only to my self, but conspicuously in my hiding. All of my so-called "doing" is nothing but my *being.* My use of my every organ of expression bespeaks my inventive mental activity. Without that insight my self expression, "Don't just do something, sit there!" may contain far more of my self appreciation than my conventional "Don't just sit there, do something!" With his poetic vigor Goethe offered conversation as the test of civilization. Surely when each conversationist knows that he can speak and listen *only* to his self, without digression, he thereby establishes the indispensable climax of self consciousness for his sane conversing.

As stated before, I can always find my present meaning for any word I use by free associating upon it, exactly as I would upon a dream element to discover what it *now* means. Once I master this process important deductions explicating life appreciation flow from it. Specifically I develop a certain way of feeling my individuality closely as a complete whole, of sensing entirety in my self identity, somewhat as the painter senses his portrait on his canvas, or the sculptor his statue in his stone. The only direction I can give my self for cultivating this magnificence is to take pains to *be my self consciously,* my *only* duty, but one that is heavy with lifelong demand for most specific self discipline, namely: *conscious self discipline in self consciousness.*

The nice point involved here is: discipline is not the same as conscious discipline, namely, what I alone *will* my self to experience. I may succeed in realizing that my military authority is entirely my own and thus experience military discipline as merely my conscious self discipline, and that likelihood would be a rare but rewarding personal achievement of conscious self integration.

Everyone considers that he knows what his language is. And everyone is right. Furthermore, only he can know, including invent, anything at all about his language. My experience teaches me that the neglect of this one linguistic fact is most common and most costly. For example, only culminating discovery and respect for its basic truth can force me as a speech researcher heedfully to find, rather than heedlessly to overlook, my mind in my work.

For example, the same essential structure framed on three foundations integrates all forms of my completed composition, beginning with my sentence onward. First, what the assertion is about (subject), second the statement of the assertion (predicate), and third the declared or undeclared *who* that is creating his subject and predicate. The last named is of greatest importance for my maintaining my conscious mental balance.

The style of my writing is intentionally unintelligible for my reader who assumes that he can read it without authoring it. I know I cannot communicate at all, ever. "Do it my self," is the humanizing spirit underlying my consciously growing my self identity. My imbalance, imprecision, lack of uniformity, and every other writer's burden, now applies largely to my prominent wish to honor all of my literature as autobiographical. I am ever recording in the book of life, of my life. As all else of mine, I create my birthplace within me. This minding what I write I regard as "the necessity of *mind* in style" (Walter Pater).

When my words do not clearly designate selfness my style becomes artificial, and I seem to my self to be able to objectify or personify. Particularly in verbalizing the truth of linguistics it is specially indicated to honor the scientific use of words, language itself providing the naming power of science. Only my appreciation that my every speech meaning is all and only about my very own self (my world) enables me to see that my whole life is always and entirely about my own marvelous human being. My factitiously denying the right to be of this, or of any other proposition, has the costly consequence of my ignoring some of my very own personal identity. It is when I know *I* am doing both the talking and listening that I waste the fewest words, including the least energy.

Hegel's saying, "Only the spirit is real," expresses the viewpoint of the student of the mind who does not unwittingly change the subject of his study.[10] As J. S. Haldane succinctly declared, "There is no escape from the conclusion that behind the appearances of a physical or biological world we are in presence of a psychological or spiritual world."[11] James Rowland Angell defined the fundamental method of psychology as "the direct examination of one's own mental processes." He concluded: "the feeling of selfhood is the very core of our psychical being. . . . However much a critical philosophy may shake our confidence in the implication of the feeling, the fact of its existence is for each of us the one absolutely indubitable fact."[12] Appreciation for the truth of this feeling is sufficient to

---

[10] *Das Geistige allein ist das Wirkliche.*
[11] *The Sciences and Philosophy,* New York: Doubleday Doran and Co., 1930.
[12] *Psychology,* New York: Henry Holt and Co., 1906.

excite the sense of unity of every life experience and self discovery.

My feeling What-there-is-in-it-for-me of any event I live suffices to excite my imagination to its creativity called *inspiration*. This conscious self awakening discovers my opportunity *everywhere* in my living, whenever I am simply ready to recognize that it is mine to turn to my conscious advantage, to serve my conscious purpose. A most striking case in point is my deliberately quickening my present mind for producing my feeling of self consciousness so that I can now write on this subject, by awakening my self awareness and observing whatever *I* am experiencing as constituting a particular treatment or aspect of my general conception of language consciousness. My acute consciousness for my self is necessary to arouse my feeling unity of my self identity with whatever I am immediately experiencing.

Either my mind's passing from its recognizable daydreaming to vigilant self consciousness, or from its unrecognizable daydream of its so-called external world to alert self consciousness, —either process is sufficient to enable creative invention of some new emotional aspect of my currently dominant interest. This method of working my mind to originate new production in the direction of my devotion provides me with an unfailing source of fresh subject content.

Every psychology of language is expressed in a language of psychology. Subjectivity is all that can be, for clearly individuality can consist of nothing else, and everything and everybody is all and only its own individual being. Objectivity or externality (that is, *outside* of subjectivity) implies nonexistence. Only by pursuing my wittingly and willingly owning every word of my varied individuality in workman-like way can I live up to my innovating self and redeem conscious truth from discredited self power. My each name-meaning is only and all of whatever *it* is, an emotional unit of my word-world. Its designation force exists entirely in itself, as an individuation of my individuality. Accurate usage of my language then is for *conscious-self* wording. Language is a person's self naming propensity necessarily consisting entirely of the selfness of the namer, whether or not the namer can feel this fact. In every instance its autonomy is integral to that of its individual linguist, whether the linguist can believe it or not. As might be expected my Alfred North Whitehead scored the vital consequence of the *whole* truth,

> To know the truth partially is to distort the Universe. . . . An unflinching determination to take the whole evidence into account is the only method of preservation against the fluctuating extremes of fashionable opinion.

MY LINGUA FRANCA

Whenever by small grammatical negligences the energy of an idea can be condensed, or a word may be made to stand for a sentence, I hold grammatical rigor in contempt.

Thomas Jefferson

Naming, a pointing and grasping activity designating and claiming independent localized individuality (emotion of meaning) is the essential linguistic movement (function). Furthermore, it is necessary to understand and practice this particularly intense process of self realization in order to achieve *insightful* wording. I need to keep heeding that my "conventional" usage of terms heavily weights them with both materiality and objectivity,—each only illusion. Even so, it is ordinarily unnecessary for me to depart from my common misusage of words if I precede such passages with my lifesavingly practical word *my.* The utility of that precious possessive pronoun is indispensable for my keeping awake to my self, despite the invitations to somnolence in the rest of my impersonal, objective, dispassionate terminology. It makes winged words out of pedestrian ones, and often romance out of lifelessness. An enheartening self encounter in my scientific literature is the rare scientist who vents his enthusiasm for his adventure of discovery in naturally picturesque prose, a Kepler, a Darwin, a Freud. My reader must *imagine* his understandable reading after all, and his author's vivid imagery is a kindness.

Edward Sapir points out that one sees and hears and otherwise experiences very largely as he does on account of the language habits of his community. My ordinary language (spoken or written) has become hardly recognizable by me as the naming of my subjective or spiritual power which it actually is. By means of my own vocabulary I can seem to subject my self to my words instead of seeing my every word as a marvelous exclamation of my strongly felt appreciation for my great peacefulness of unity. How beautifully Cardinal John

81

Henry Newman (*Idea of a University Defined,* 1873) worded his lament: "Alas! What are we doing all through life, both as a necessity and as a duty, but unlearning the world's poetry, and attaining to its prose!" Obligation lies on me to support the seeming of my impassioned unpopularity whenever the conscious unity of my *being* is at stake. What else is it to be a manly man! I confront only my self. Any other seeming confrontation depends entirely upon my dislocating some of my own living.

I find my sanity to issue from my ability to see good naturedly the ideal helpfulness in *every* passage of human activity. Connotation of kindness therefore provides practical utility that must always be present, clear, and central in my wording of my living, if I would have it be lovably livable. Regardless of the mood I verbalize, if it is a passion I can emote self consciously in the literary service, my composition shows that its animus is subject to me (rather than I to it), for example, by using a whole vocabulary of disparaging terms, yet maintaining a congruous emotional level of understanding "to give the devil his due." Sometimes mere understatement is enough to attain this effect of a contented mind working with its feelings of discontent. (Litotes serves additional purpose of revealing the affirmation hidden in negation).

It is the inescapable law of my psychology that I cannot use my words for the purpose of communication or of communion, but that I can and must use them for the purpose of honoring my own organic *union.* A close look at my rhythmic pleasure in communication or in communion reveals its truth to be my enjoyment of my United Self. Recorded great man of letters, Emerson, "Union is within. . . . Union must be ideal in actual individualism." Susanne K. Langer made this point, "The essence of language is symbolic, not signific; we use it first and most vitally to formulate and hold ideas in our own minds." She describes the young child just learning to speak as always talking to his self.

Only *consciously self learned* behavior can contribute to appreciation for the wholeness of self. My language grows with

my need to function, to use my power of pure and intense iden-
tification with my diction. Hence it is vitally meaningful to be
able to conceive of one's language as a product of his learning.
My chief concern in my reading, writing, speaking, or listening
about any scientific theme is to identify my self convincingly
with my truth that it is all and only about me. This practical
ideal dominating my writing is of the greatest helpfulness to
organic me in my all-important concern of "keeping my head
on my shoulders," not seeming to "lose my mind," "studying
my head on rather than off," not "getting off my base," and
just "hanging on to my self." It is just exactly this practical
service that I imagine my reader is always needing to offer his
self, but nevertheless resisting from his lifelong habit of withholding it in the name of modesty, humility, even unworthiness,
or whatever rationalization of his unconscious practice of self-
belittlement-through-self-unconsciousness.

To gain control over my use of my words and learn to appreciate them as my literary self only, I must practice constant
vigilance in my everyday talk and listening, as well as in my
writing and reading, to make sure that I am *disciplining* my
self in terms of heeding my self identity only in it all. Justly
thus can I make my tongue or pen honor my truth. In this literary exertion I must ever respect the fact that *all of my self
disregard is only in the service of regard for the extent of my
self I can already appreciate as such.*

Conscious fidelity to my deeply felt truth of the absoluteness
of my inviolable subjectivity has completely eliminated my
need for such dualities as public and private, impersonal and
personal, you and I, and the like, each depending for its existence upon my consciously disowning some aspect of my living.

Every individual can live only his own individual world,
therefore everyone can and *must* create his only possible world
language, and further, I prefer that everyone of my government, my UN, and my UNESCO know it! Plato defined social
justice as minding one's own business. My every term that
appears to "present" anything else is fundamentally a *symbol*
of my individuality. However, as long as this insight remains to

be developed, I must unwittingly continue to cultivate only my own world language without being able to admit it. I cannot then acknowledge that my measured life is all and only about my metrical self. Such admitted self responsibility would be irreconcilable with my choice of language which appears plainly to state that my life is not merely all about my self, but that rather it seems mostly about everything and everybody else instead!

Further self disregard issues from my habitual feeling that I have had nothing to do personally with the building up of my own vocabulary. The attraction of "hip lingo" of the slum-living child is that it enables him to survive in a closed ghetto. According to John Brewer, assistant director of compensatory education for the City of Pittsburgh, this "hidden language" is a protective device which provides the child with critically needed "feeling of unity, a oneness." Mr. Brewer has "compiled a list of 5,000 slum idioms . . . the product of creativity and imagination."[1]

For the good of his whole world, it is the most critical of all services of my linguist to discipline his emotionality to be able to feel the vitality of his language. It is far more important that I know just what I *can* talk about than that I take for granted that I can talk about something or somebody other than that. Appreciation for the full freedom of my mind is an issue of knowing that all of it *is* mine. Walter Savage Landor sensitively remarked a literary distribution of rich self ardor, "Prose on certain occasions can bear a great deal of poetry; on the other hand, poetry sinks and swoons under a moderate weight of prose." There can be no interest but self interest, but consciousness for that truth varies in my life. It is apt to be wanting when my wish to be matter-of-fact becomes stronger than my wish to realize that I am the only matter of my every fact. A chief motive of my experience with poetic diction is apt to be recognizable as conscious self exaltation. As a rule my studied prose does not aim at this elevation, but when it does it reflects my conscious subjectivity.

[1] *The Detroit News,* August 24, 1966, 22A.

Words of subdued emotion which may benumb my precious sense of self possession impoverish my enjoyment of the dignity and power of my human being. It cannot be appreciated too much: my every pejorative word obstructs my self appreciation by appearing to detract from the true excellence of my living. My every negation obstructs my self insight by appearing to assert: Something of me, is not. Every affirmation is life affirming; every negation is life negating.

Entity is unity, is individuality. Biological observation attests man is constantly growing new selfness in his cultivating his individuality. *In toto* he may be conceived as a normal neoplastic development of his humanness and until he appreciates this nature of his augmenting wholeness he disrespects healthful truth of his constitution. As he creates his mental condition of seeming divisiveness, instead of unity, he imposes analogous necessity upon his physiological order with consequent evidence of one or another apparent disorder, such as organ dysfunction or abnormal neoplasm which does not seem to him to be made up entirely of his own living. His words fixate mental attitudes of disowned integration, when they do not free his meanings for building up his appreciation for the cadence of the advancement of his literary identity. This insight is not alien to the physician: "No surgeon can observe and treat many patients with cancer without realizing the tremendous emotional impact of the word 'cancer' itself upon its victims. . . . This anxiety is an inherent feature of the disease, and is a vital consideration in the total care of these patients."[2]

Particularly in the study of my rhetoric must I heed that I live under constant obligation to distinguish my every device of composition as standing all and only for my mighty life's meaning. My cultivation of a grammatical habit of mind must not preclude my worthy devotion to my self consciousness. My lucidity for my life appreciation is my primary concern, and by seeking other organic development first I ruin consciousness

[2] John S. Stehlin, Jr., M.D. and Kenneth H. Beach, "Psychological Aspects of Cancer Therapy, A Surgeon's Viewpoint," *Journal of the American Medical Association*, July 11, 1966, Vol. 197, No. 2.

for the Owndom of God that is naturally mine. My immediate responsibility is that of learning to renounce semantic terms as well as other habits that obstruct my observing that the world I live is the world I name, that the world my fellowman lives is the world he names, and finally, that the only possible language must be each individual's world language.

Emerson, who esteemed his poetic power as highest, declared, "The poet is the sayer, the namer, and represents a little beauty. . . . He is the true and only doctor. . . . The people fancy they hate poetry, and they were all poets and mystics. . . . The poets made all of the words. . . . The religions of the world are the ejaculations of a few imaginative men." And how ideally Wordsworth defended the stanza form and described its value in his "Sonnet on the Sonnet":

> Scorn not the Sonnet; Critic, you have frowned,
> Mindless of its just honors; with this key
> Shakespeare unlocked his heart; the melody
> Of this small lute gave ease to Petrarch's wound;
> A thousand times this pipe did Tasso sound;
> With it Camöens soothed an exile's grief;
> The Sonnet glittered a gay myrtle leaf
> Amid the cypress with which Dante crowned
> His visionary brow: a glow-worm lamp,
> It cheered mild Spenser, called from Faery-land
> To struggle through dark ways; and, when a damp
> Fell round the path of Milton, in his hand
> The Thing became a trumpet; whence he blew
> Soul-animating strains—alas, too few!

My language is organic, instinct with marvelous life, full of life's action, and is never fixed with the stillness or sameness of undeveloping meaning. I preserve my unanimity, and further my self understanding, by preserving my linguistic freedom. It is life relevant that I have confidence in my self rather than in a dictionary. Poised upon my self I can appreciate the importance of my meaning for any word. I can find that meaning only by free associating around it, as noted. To my question, "What then is the good of a dictionary if I do not believe in the finality of its definitions?" I reply, "My dictionary, quite as all of my reading, is most helpful as a reliable source for my enriching and exciting my word life, for my cultivating my free associating, for my appreciating my self world."[3]

William von Humboldt stated that language cannot be regarded as a substance which is always present. It is an organic process which must constantly be produced. Observance of this truth, namely, my language *is* my organic being, is most realistic support for my realizing that it is self relevant only. Presumably, my wordage consisting only of my own mind's organicity, I may expect to be able to derive knowledge of the working of my mind from my philological and etymological research.

Using this linguistic approach to my psychology it is desirable that the name I give to any of my psychic processes be one that signifies its personal holistic nature. To be sure it would be similarly individuality-respecting if my nomination of every anatomical, biochemical, or physiological element denote due respect for my solipsistic nature. Present scientific nomenclature for my organic constitution uses eponyms freely, leaving me completely anonymous.

Even my health struggles may be experienced under a name other than my own, e.g., Parkinson, Thomsen, Graves, Osler, and so on. When I am enduring any health trial, I need to mobilize all of my strength and under my own name. Therefore the name of any life process may well be expected to imply its organic principle founded upon its organic wholeness, so that a person can recognize his identity in it. I need above all to have my vocabulary contribute to my sense of my completeness. The fuller my conscious self knowledge the fuller my self understanding. Understanding anything is the feeling that its existence is just.

When man observes his self as beginning and end for his self

---

[3] The extreme behaviorist would regard language as a complex system of motor habits, and systematic thinking as merely implicit motor or glandular activity involving language mechanisms. Such explanation is pointful in its way, stressing individuality as it does.

he can mobilize the motivation to use his language to further his appreciation for his living. Henry Ward Beecher, criticized for grammatical errors in his sermon, commented, "Young man, when the English language gets in my way, it doesn't stand a chance."

The claim is often made that the great theories of Newton, Darwin or Freud become schoolboy property in the age succeeding, that great discoveries of research get eventual access to the common mind by the work of lecturer, textbook, or now modern audio-visual aids. This claim, dreamy and necessarily inaccurate, obviously derives from the wish for the development of some kind of common sense inventiveness. My cultivation of my capacity for imaginative production is not the consequence of any formal educational experience. From reading all about what Newton accomplished I cannot develop his way of accomplishing. Or my Freud's "telling me" how he creates his self understanding cannot pass truly for my being able to discipline my self with self consciousness. However if I can succeed in believing that I already know what Darwin knew I can spare my self the arduous effort of really cultivating my proficiency in that direction. Only when my whole mental attitude is infused with the spirit of pursuing self understanding, as my Freud's was, then I may safely dare to expect sometime to be able to use my mind as he seemed to use his.

I surely believe in the existence of "an external world," but my belief is based upon evidence which I find all and only in my self, and of course that evidence indicates the existence of *subjectivity* (not objectivity) other than my own. But I can grow my language in such a self distracted way that I can hardly feel the truth that my every word *is* the issue of my own choice. Then my language can, so to speak, appear to take over my psychology.

To modify my W. J. Turner's assertion: Anything is its own cause, and the cause of anything is its own everything.[4] Only strict individuality consciousness can bring out clearly the irreconcilable contradiction in causal dependency (deter-

---

[4] Anything has a cause, and the cause of anything is everything.

minism). Everything *is* its own everything. No meaning of mine can exist apart from me, for it is all and only a specific use of my self. Truth and number one are inseparable.[5]

My apparent quibbling about my words is really a curbing of my tendency to linguistic laxity. My self unconsciousness actively supports my disregarding my real and great need for conscious self culture. My spirit of self observation is completely identical with my scientific spirit, each gathering facts (truths, data) from my own experiencing (living) them. My discipline of keeping the senses of my mind consciously mine is essential for my being able to acknowledge my originality, my self reliant creativity. I now realize that being fully awake involves my self interest only. Self alert Plato sensed: Whosoever seeks, knows that which he seeks for in general notion; else how shall he know when he has found it?

---

[5] Pythagorean assertion: number is the truth of being. My student punned, "Determinism would deter monism."

MY CREATIVE READING

What do you read, my lord?—Polonius.
Words, words, words.—Hamlet.

To observe my sensing and perceiving as entirely my own mental activity is essential for my beholding all of my observation as being my own mental creation only. Right there is where I must call upon my use of my senses to go beyond what is ordinarily considered to be sufficient performance. I have not developed fully any of my sensory functioning until I can believe the evidence of my senses as self evidence. I have not learned the full use of my eyes until I realize what I am seeing is a scene in my mind; of my ears until I realize what I am hearing is sound in my mind; what I am touching until I realize what I touch is felt in my mind; and so on throughout all of my mind's sensory experience. Whenever I "consider the source" fully I end up with conscious self consideration.

To avoid language trouble it helps me to keep heeding that *my* every somebody or something else really *is* all and only mine. Otherwise, at consistent cost to my appreciation for *my* single mindedness, I assert that I can be I and also not-I. My every word, term, name, or vocal utterance of any kind is a quiddity of my real subjective *momentary existence* only, and it needs my distinct evaluation as such to contribute to my conscious self potentiation. However, this truth is difficult to put to words for word unconsciousness supports rigid formalism of self unconsciousness. Nevertheless it is one's sanest educational goal. Self wise Randolph S. Bourne (*Youth and Life,* 1913) disposed and steadied his mind to feel "discipline does not mean being moulded by outside forces, but sticking to one's road against the forces that would deflect or bury the soul." And, "Much of our early education was as automatic and unconscious as the handing down of the immemorial traditions in a primitive savage tribe." From lack of an accurate vision of my self I fall into the view of making a living, rather than of living my making. Adds Bourne, "That self-recognition, which is the only basis for a genuine spiritual success in life, is the thing that too many of us lack."[1]

Application of this comprehensive view of generative individuality to the stutterer's speech therapy (loving renunciation of his habit of stuttering) is obvious. His recourse to his stuttering varies in direct proportion with his recourse to considering that he can get at someone else and that someone else can hear him or observe him in some way. His growing his true view of his intact unique allness and its associated insight that one can only speak (or listen) to one's self, is accompanied by freedom from his fear of alien control reflected in his insecure voice. Stuttering is a helpful but painful byproduct of the life-endangering illusion, communication. It may be gradually dispelled by each successive realization of the stutterer that all of his speech, including his hearing, is, and must be, only his completely self contained self expression.

Conscious self tolerance results from seeing to it that the ground of my acknowledgeable self estimate is not merely bound by my ability to feel pleasure or pain but rather extended by cultivating my capacity for universality of taste. By painstakingly enlarging my interests I pursue a life course of conscious self fulfilment. My taking the trouble to verify that my every experience *is* my self experience is necessary training in and for accurate observation. This exaction lets my verbalized emotion (that is, my thinking) attain its full growth.

My persistent demand for ordaining my experience with conscious self appreciation is the foundation for my realizing my originality in my speaking or writing. It always leads to my energizing confidence in my doing my own living, in my feeling my literary style is my own human style. In *The Working Principles of Rhetoric* (1900) mind-feeling John Franklin Genung mentions of literary work:

> ... much had better be left to that strange power which the mind has of working subconsciously. In many cases when the train of thought is started . . . the best way is to leave it to itself, and when

[1] *Youth and Life,* Boston: Houghton Mifflin Co., 1913.

92

next the subject is recalled a remarkable advance and clearing-up will be found to have taken place . . . this because the whole mind has been engaged on it, and produced a growth rather than a manufacture.

As I close the gap between my use of words and my conscious self, all of my unconscious need for helpful (but distressful) symptoms of self repudiation comes to light. What explains the all too obvious fact that communication does *seem* possible, is that each so-called communicator *is* making sense by personally experiencing *all* of the incommunicable that he can mean by communication. His defense of his illusion of communication is all and only his self defense. He indulges this illusion of speech magic to cover up his consciously rejected, but unconsciously continuing, individual *integrity*.

Most feared of all self orientations is the only possible true one: naked, unadorned *solipsism*. This utmost life revering *self alone* orientation to divine human being, is by definition completely unpopular, incapable of demonstration except to one's solipsistic self, and fiercely rejected as false and dangerous by every well intentioned communer who has not yet worked up his individuality appreciation sufficiently to be able to call his soul his own and his all his soul. I can readily find my fellowman who has worked up his self insight to appreciate his bountiful being for its true self sufficiency. He is always the conscious-mind working one who staunchly safeguards his attention from being distracted to any less self respecting life attitude. It is his trusted way of not deserting any theme, by allowing it to develop itself. He purposefully keeps one topic, or more, growing itself in his unconscious mind. Maxwell Irving Pitkin, named "epicurean word-chiseler" by his friend and printer, Oliver A. Wallace, writes:[2]

> Formal composition, for most scribes, is better done on paper where the elusive phrase is permanently recorded, the fugitive word captured, the form and cadence of the thing made obvious to the eye.

[2] *Words,* Edinburgh: Oliver Press, 1932, pp. 15 and 16, and p. 46.

Yet, in another sense, mental composition has been habitual with all great writers who have been generous enough to disclose their habits of thought.

They instinctively think in words. Under the elm tree, along the trout stream, even in the thoroughfares and work shops of life, they are coining phrases, silently casting what they think and see into appropriate language, fitting and discarding adjective and verb in the eternal search for perfect expression.

Freckled newsboys, sunsets, traffic jams, symphonies, even the abstract meditations of reverie, pass into their minds as phrases, to sink, apparently forgotten, into the store-house of the unconscious mind.

When such men sit down to write they have no need to brush the cobwebs from a neglected vocabulary. The joints of expression are not stiff and squeaky from long disuse.

They have spun the glorious skein in wayward hours, and when loom-time comes there remains only the weaving of the pattern. . . . Thoughts go blowing through your head that are wiser than your own—vagrant inspirations that bubble suddenly up from the impenetrable surface of your subconscious mind, sparkle for a moment, and burst, and disappear.

Moments of inspiration—flashes of genius—plain happy thoughts—call them what you will. But if you are wise you will honor them as the finest flower of your thinking. And you will take the pains to write them down before they dissolve into forgetfulness.

All of my speaking and writing can only express sure self-ness. Emerson ever reveres self, "Whoso would be a man must be a nonconformist. He who would gather immortal palms must not be hindered by the name of goodness, but must explore if it be goodness. Nothing is at last sacred but the integrity of your own mind." Thus every comprehensively self feeling man finds it necessary to exalt man to God.

Obviously, full devotion to his solipsistic wholeness must be, and can only be, the wonderful understanding of the individual who has *painstakingly* discovered it by, about, and for his self. By definition, all that passes for one's formal education (teaching of knowledge to a pupil by an educator) must, and can only, obscure its magnificent reality as being too awesome to consider soberly.

If I marshal a spirited defense of use of language as a means of verbal "intercourse," it would only reflect my dependence upon it for my unrecognizable way of disguising my true solipsistic nature. To be, is to be expressed, and I *must* express my allness, although I may deceive myself by asserting that some of it is not-I. Then my seeming communication with my not-I, is my symptom with which I can ignore the unity of my inviolable individuality by attributing a magic power of unification (uniting I and not-I) to my language. The only possible way to accomplish what is meant by uniting men is through each individual man's seeing his self as united, seeing he *is* whatever he lives and names his fellowman. My language of recognized and esteemed subjectivity is the only one which allows me to realize that I am using it rather than seeming to be used by it.

Emerson felt the necessity, "One must be an inventor to read well. . . . There is then creative reading as well as creative writing." This means that my mind reads the inventive lines of its author by feeling my identity in whatever I read; by making my self conscious for the truth that what I read I am creating through my intentionally living it as a growth process in my mind. Such creative reading, made possible by my self consciousness, is distinguished by my feeling my enlivening self interest. This literary orientation is scored by Emerson in "The American Scholar": "I had better never see a book than to be warped by its attraction clean out of my own orbit and made a satellite instead of a system. The one thing in the world, of value, is the active soul."

It is with this appreciation for creative reading that Francis Bacon wrote in his essay "Of Studies": "A good Book is the pretious life-blood of a master spirit, imbalm'd and treasur'd up on purpose to a life beyond life."

My own conscious living of what I read, in science as in any romance, dispenses with the whole notion of escape literature as it creates its excitement characteristic for its adventurous experience. In "Men and Books," Austin Phelps (1820–1890) affirmed the value to the individual of creative reading:

> . . . the method is supported by the practice of many eminent authors. . . . With great variety of tastes, successful authors have

generally agreed in availing themselves of this natural and facile method of educating their minds to the work of original creation.

For me creative reading consciously applies not only to the speciality I am studying but also to *all* that I read, for all that I read is literally a new becoming of my own living. To illustrate this consciously-working feeling, only by the creative reading of my daily newspaper can I succeed in feeling my identity in the variety of emotionality *that* experience presents. Thus to consider my newspaper a kind of diary of my personal world is to cultivate the ideally practical civic spirit. Without this mind-broadening experience I tend to view my world events impersonally, that is, irresponsibly.

My concentrated feeling that I am being what I am reading is a crucial test of the strength of my conscious self love, *all* of my prejudice being nothing but my unacknowledgeable self intolerance protecting the *status quo* of my present conscious personal identity. My self conscious professional experience helps me most to diagnose and treat my patient as my self. In my lecturing in psychiatry *I am my psychotic, neurotic, perverted, or otherwise "sociopathic" patient.*

Disciplining my feeling my identity deeply and amplifying it broadly while reading, I cultivate my mind with liberal and liberating self education. In his *Yale Lectures,* Nathaniel Judson Burton (1822–1887) states:

> I have been surprised many times, after I have diligently gestated a subject myself and then have started out into my library for the say-so of other men on that subject, to notice not merely in what a lightsome and expert way I handle them, but also in what a swift facility I utilized their many volumes. . . . Almost any man may make the experiment for himself.

For me the vital issue here is my initiatory apprehension of the theme of this volume, namely, that I feel and avow my own original unity, my vital wholeness, in *my creating* of my say-so of other men. This concentration suggests to me Joseph Joubert's (1754–1824) literary problem (*Thoughts,* p. 275), "If there be a man tormented by the cursed ambition to put a whole book into a page, a whole page into a phrase, and that phrase into a word, I am that man." My conscious solipsism is my one and only workable life orientation that fits my Edmund Burke (1729–1797) in his self justifying proposition of peace as he developed it in his "Speech on Conciliation with America" (1775): "Not Peace through the medium of war; . . . It is Peace sought in the spirit of Peace; and laid in principles purely pacific."

If all of *my* writing (or reading) necessarily is autobiographical, why should I take any pains to make it rhetorical? On account of the fact that *I* want it to be as readable (creational) as possible by *my* reader. All of my good manners is my effort to please my self, in my choosing my general composure as in my arranging this composition. As a rule, I find that my reader's objection to his author's style, regularly turns on his resisting its steadfast insistence that every individual is necessarily, either consciously or unconsciously, the responsible creator of his every read, heard, written, or spoken word.

To apprehend is to originate. Literary endeavor involves choosing and arranging readily creational diction. I regard my *persevering* reader as always in the attitude of willingly originating his author's literary sentiment as his own. He must be the rare one who is already cultivating his marvelous aptitude for his conscious life appreciation. Obviously this solipsistic requirement disqualifies a literary production from becoming popular.

A certain danger always exists in writing over the head of or writing down to one's reader. However, just as a writer's description of seeing cannot bring vision to his blind fellowman, similarly his account of self sight cannot bring self awareness to his reader who has not cultivated this power. My skilful workmanship in language may be expected to flourish with my working up my sense of self identity.

A modern scientist's most troublesome tendency may be his limited ability to read his strictly personal biography into all of his scientific literature. In his scientific writing a whole-self revering scientist can intentionally suppress his mind's consciousness. He might do this out of respect for his expected scientific reader who has displaced his own sense of his personal identity upon his unobserved working of his mind which he soulfully and studiously calls impersonal science.

However, *whatever* is lived by a human being really must contain humanity's precious, all-sufficing warrant of *individuality*. Whatever he thinks, *is* rational for him. All of his reality *is* hypostatized mentality. All of his mentality *is* entirely his own living of it. Whatever he feels, *is* biologically adequate. Whatever his mind produces, *is* wisdom. Whatever he asserts, *is* true of him. His world *is* his private universe. His creed *is* belief in his self. His freely functioning love of his living excites his self consciousness. His doctrine is his mind observation. His law is his human constitution. His freedom is his voluntary self control. His subjectivity is his spirit. His divinity is his godliness. There is no retreating to his subjective sphere for there is no leaving it. There is nothing for him to forget or remember, for his present living is all that he can live. Thus, he has *no other* ground for human welfare or culture than that of his immediate self interest or self devotion. And his most helpful linguistic possession is exact word definition, plain and direct, which features this vital truth: his every word can be only a present name for his own life's power. His own purposeful behavior reveals itself as empowered by its own cause.

I dwell, as now, most monotonously, upon the *naming* significance of every word on account of the *importance* of my awareness for my own self identity. I find that my disciplined development of my ability to feel my own self identity is necessary for me to be able to attribute self identity in my world-at-large. Conversely, I find that incompetence in my ability to appreciate my self identity *as enlarging itself* leads to corresponding irresponsibility in my conduct of my living of my fellowman.

As might be expected, I find that what has held together my delusion, the external world, is my auxiliary delusion, communication. Thus intercourse, conversation, sympathy, and analogous names connoting plurality appear to be able to compensate me for my not calling *my* soul entirely my own and *my* experience entirely my soul's freedom to be all its own. *I can never express my self in any other way or from any other motive than to save my life, my very owndom.* Any sound which I cannot recognize as a variant of my own name is my undeveloped vocalism. Quite as Theodore Simon Jouffroy (1792–1842) described his conscious self love, "Liberty is the ideal of the me."

Every word of this declared idiolect of individuality must be the product of each one's *disciplined* creative imagination. I have discovered conscious idiolect to be my, hence my mankind's, most distressing desideratum. Working it up painstakingly is the most helpful scientific use of my imagination, providing the acknowledgeable lifeblood of all that I name science. Without it I can collect dispassionate fact but I cannot make or record lovable discovery. With it I illuminate all of my research with the practical sunlight of enlightened self interest. It, and it only, can reveal the specific beauty of my scientific ideal. *The real beauty of well-made language that I name my Science of Self is felt in what it tells me, including my fellowman, of the nature of divine living itself.*

I wish to mention one of countless historic instances of the spiritual cost of ignored literary vitality. Self wise Edwin P. Whipple naming Charles Brockden Brown (1771–1810) the first American novelist by profession states:[3] "Brown in his depth of insight into the morbid phenomena of the human mind, really anticipated Hawthorne. . . . Brown is one of the most melancholy instances of a genius arrested in its orderly development by the pressure of circumstances . . . sacrificing every grace and felicity of style to the inexorable need of writing rapidly, and therefore inaccurately . . . to make what is called 'a living'."

All of my sensibility is aesthetic and any recognition of my science as cultivating my life-affirming self appreciation sud-

[3] *American Literature,* Boston: Ticknor and Co., 1887, p. 28. John Greenleaf Whittier thus described his Whipple, "With the possible exception of Lowell and Matthew Arnold, he was the ablest critical essayist of his time."

denly provides me with demonstration of an unfailing source of aesthetic satisfaction. To create scientific discovery is the scientist's way of putting on "the new man." My invention is my individuality's enjoying an access of conscious being. No fact can be worthy except in the sense of being lifeworthy, manworthy. *And conscious worth is the greatest good of man, for he can be interested in taking care of his life only in direct proportion to the conscious value he places upon it.* Lifeless finding never presents itself to the mind of the discoverer. Never can an observation be made that does not consist entirely and only of the living of the observer.

Of consciously compelling interest to me as an observer is what I name my "observation" which is nothing but my *observing.* Furthermore my observing can be nothing but another name for my very life process itself, which is all that *can* ever be of any real interest to me whatsoever. I do well to regard every term (word) that does not name (call my attention to) my self, as a barbarous one subserving my self's disregard, hence my life's depreciation. I *live* whatever is for me. It is all ever true. My language of recognizable self helps me to make it *consciously* true.

SUMMARY

A perfect Judge will read each work of Wit
With the same spirit that its author writ:
Survey the Whole, nor seek slight faults to find
Where nature moves, and rapture warms the mind.

Pope

As far as its importance for furthering my life appreciation is concerned, the consequence of my language is specifically and solely a matter of whether and how much I live its impassioned power as subject to me or live my self as subject to it. If I bother my self about it at all, I readily acknowledge that my own language often carries me far beyond my conscious control, readily leading me both to say what I do not mean and to mean what I do not say. This state of confusion of my linguistic affairs obtains, beyond shockingly few of my tried and true conscious self verbalizations. Self wordy as my contribution to my literature may appear to me, I find it also my vigorous condensation of its lifesaving theme. It is my conscious language of my three score and ten years that tells of my mind's current working. I cannot "boil it down" while I am boiling with it. I write only for and to my self and do not wish to conceal my painful truth in the name of my pleasant prejudice. Moncure Daniel Conway (1832–1907) in his *Idols and Ideals* recorded this spirited sentiment:[1]

> The free inquirer will discover full soon that the only "saving faith" is a perfect trust in truth, and that the only real infidelity is the belief that a lie can do better work than truth. He will take to heart Montaigne's advice, and fear only Fear. . . . St. Gregory felt sorrow to be a capital sin.

Certainly I renounce my not-I living just exactly as fast and far as I can consciously feel my self identity. Just as certainly,

[1] *Idols and Ideals*, New York: Henry Holt and Co., 1877, pp. 150, 157.

101

when I experience any living in which I cannot consciously feel my self, I observe my tendency to fill up all such events with my illusion of not-self. It is only by taking pains that I can wish "whatever will happen" for my fellowman, so strong is my habit of believing in so-called well-wishing. On the other hand, I am able to help my self realistically in the sense that well-wishing itself constitutes a form of realization of spiritual benefit.

Furthermore the master reach of my linguistic habit is very great so that I feel dismayed by the idea of struggling to renounce it lovingly. Also I tend to consider my word-power as I do my hand or foot, as an unconscious growth of my self that I must henceforth make the best of. The actuality is that I can, if I will work at it, learn to make my word-power serve my conscious will, strengthen my hold on my life, develop my due sense of self esteem and, by developing my capacity for living consciously, enable my self to enjoy my really wonderful individuality ever creating my marvelous self world. Even my dispassionate annalist is really a *passionate self analyst.*

This self respecting view, that my language is nothing but my conscious creation which I can make over in any way to suit *my* real nature and needs, is obscured by my limited self consciousness. Thus my language may contribute to my limiting the range of my self awareness, which in turn may favor my developing my language of dangerously limited self regard.

Present popular or traditional literary style encourages a writer to personify unconsciously whatever he may not regard as his own living and to depersonalize consciously whatever he might see as his own. Apart from duly acknowledged autobiography, only the most intrepidly sincere individualist dares to record his observation that all of his language is and must be merely his very own exclusively personal wording of his purely selfish interests, that his every vocable can have its only meaning just for his entirely private subjective world of his self. Any and all language that I do not use to reveal my self to my self, I use only to conceal my self from my self.

Moncure Daniel Conway poses this historic issue:

The royal sensualist, surrounded by his concubines, and jaded with luxury, exclaimed, "There is nothing new under the sun!" The seer on Patmos, exiled and lonely, cried, "I see a new heaven and a new earth!" . . . I count the highest gain which philosophy has attained in this age to be the perception that the real way to reach a better world is to secure a better man.

Individual consciousness, Conway soliloquized, is

the pregnant fact that is able to preserve a continuous existence and identity through all the appreciable changes of form, and to survive the departure of many bodies. A man of seventy-five has possessed at least ten different bodies; these have come from nature to invest his personality and been successively yielded back to nature; yet the man feels himself one and the same mind that acted in well-remembered scenes when he was a child.

It is my not-I mentality that demands exercise in my illusions of objectivity and of externality. It is my not-I mentality out of which I construct all of my impersonal imaginings such as my society or government or school or race or mob or crowd or any so-called organization.

Right now as I write, throughout my beloved United States everyone is paying dearly for indulging in his illusion called race, unable to realize that *it* is completely incapable of any kind of behavior whatsoever. Race is only a name for an abstraction that has *all* of its existence entirely and only in the mind of the human individual creating and using it. But this reality orientation about the true meaning of one's every word (meaning that is emotion resident only in the mind making it) is the essence of sanity and the one sure source of thoroughly satisfying human peace and prosperity. That it is difficult and that it is human to try what seems easier, even if it does not and cannot work the desired result, —all of that is also good and true.

It has been my finding from extensive experience with my fellowman that he uses his imagination unconsciously, rather than consciously, to feel his superstition and delusion, so that he cannot control this power. My ancient Roman performed the rites of Angerona, his goddess of agony, in the temple of Volupia, his goddess of ecstasy, to denote the concealed identity in unpleasure and pleasure. Not improbably he named his Furies the Eumenides (the well-meaning) to indicate "that pain is not without its heart of good. . . . All the moral laws have been written by crimes."[2]

What is the psychology of my language that can appear to rebel against its creator, steadily undermine my understanding of my own mind by reducing it to a logomachy, and set up separate autonomies which seem to usurp and crowd out my own individual autonomy? This is precisely what my language appears to be able to do to me. I can find my self at cross-purposes, evidently in conflict with my self, under the authority of power that I cannot recognize as my own, and so on, bereft of my conscious self integrity, self love and self sovereignty, —with my language clearly describing and confirming such painful state of my affairs. Very few of my words seem to attest all that is really true of them, namely that they are merely my names for elements of my own being which I choose to invent and use. Moncure Daniel Conway felt the craving for unity to be the soul of philosophy. He finds "realizing the ideal" impractical, and "idealizing the real . . . the main secret of the art of living." He mentions a "great portrait-painter" who, asked if he did not find many faces "totally uninteresting or even repulsive," replied, "I never had to paint a face which did not possess lines and meanings beyond my power to seize and portray." Making conscious a fresh truth of my life always gives me a stronger mind to control and work.

The following question is of greatest concern for my *every* human being and is best posed until its answer becomes sun clear. Since his language is his very own word power, obviously supposed to help him understand and appreciate his very own human individuality, *why* and *how* does it happen instead that every individual finds he uses his word power chiefly to cultivate ignoration and depreciation for his really wonderful self?

For determining any truth whatsoever I am my only possible

[2] *Idols and Ideals,* pp. 164, 187.

104

court of first or last resort. With that life orientation, I find my mind strongest when it can see the good in *any* mind working of my fellowman, in brief, when it indulges no negation in order to honor its own integrity. For me, my own living is all that can ever have any certainty or uncertainty about it. Particularly ever since I dislocated my trusted parent as if outside of me my tendency is to "look out" from my self for my helpfulness whereas I can actually find it only *within* me.

The name "mystic" is given to anyone who discovers and believes in his subjectivity as the source of his truth, reality, divinity, self identity, world knowledge, or whatever he lives. The mystic always bears witness that his *conscious* self knowledge provides his mental picture of his worth, of his godliness. As may well be imagined it is rare for a writer who uses his word mystic to begin by defining it.

I lose access to a valuable sensibility for any of my living I denominate not-I. Furthermore I use up precious imagination in maintaining such repudiated selfness as if it could be an external body or world or divinity. Even more important, my conscious appreciation for my life itself diminishes as I alienate it from my conscious observation and control, by believing of my self only such evidence as I find it comfortable to believe. Louis Agassiz (1807–1873) voiced a fact of his great scientific experience: every great truth one finally appreciates is the product of 1) first his rejection, 2) then his consideration until he can accept it, and 3) finally his softly assuming that he acknowledged it from the start. My truth of the lifesaving importance of disciplining my mind continuously with consciousness for my self thus evolved.

Discovering and practicing my life-giving truth of self direction did not come as easily as finding how to use my compass. Neither can I communicate that it is the only method by which I can restore awareness for my original perfectness, innocence, and appreciation for my amazing power. One with my self is my only possible real majority.

However, lifesaving conscious self orientation must remain inaccessible to me as long as I am unable to dispel my every illusion that there is a particle of truth, except wild illusion, to be found in my popular so-called objectivity. Either I must study and practice labor-saving self realization as my way of life or forfeit appreciation for my real greatness. Either I must persevere in conscious self growth for self fulfilment or find that I cannot justify my own existence. Margaret Fuller (1810–1850) felt her truth, "if men knew how to look around them, they need not look above."

Particularly on account of its inconstant signification Thomas Hobbes (1588–1679) felt that a word is a wise man's counter, he but reckons by it; a word is only a fool's money. However it is conceivable that a vocabulary, each word standing consciously for its possessor instead of for a grammar text book, might approximate a true-to-life nature of literacy.

For my learning about life, beginning especially with my learning to talk, I found "easy going" in the well-worn path of established self misinterpretation referred to loosely and inaccurately as family living. A family can do no living whatsoever. But I cultivated my strong belief that I grew up in my family rather than that all that I could possibly mean by *my* family had to grow up in me. Similarly I indulged the illusion and delusion (of depersonalization) that I belonged to *my* home, school, church, country, and so on, rather than that all I could possibly signify by such powerful meanings really consisted of development of my own mind. I know of no person's language that does not continually suppose his world to be external to his mind, so that he must occasionally puzzle deeply over "the whichness of the what" (Bronson Alcott, 1799–1888). Yet such an apparently life remote language cannot be used without contributing to its user's increasingly indulging his own self belittlement. Enlarging self unconsciousness is the price I pay for the advancement of my knowledge that I cannot recognize as knowledge all and only about my self. Aristotle felt, "the mind may be called the eye of the soul" (*The Nicomachean Ethics*).

Following my awakening to the true state of the strictly personal nature of all of my living, I appreciated heartily a story that seemed to me to be justly descriptive of nearly every child's necessarily burdening his exquisitely tender sensibility with his family living. Standing on the seashore a man descries just a dark speck far out at sea. After a long while he can recognize it is a child, tired but determined, floating and flaying his way to land. The man swims out to help the youngster, wanting to know what had happened. The youngster explains, "Oh, my mother and father took me way out there in a boat, and left me there." "All by your self?" "Yes." "Well wasn't that very dangerous?" "Yes, it was. But the hardest part was my getting out of that sack."

I first came to my understanding of the difficult concept "brain wash" primarily by becoming insightful about the way I grew my mother and father and sibling experiences, in living my own home as if all of it had not been entirely my own self experiencing. Thus as I created my so-called common language I could not see it as a self deception system allowing me to appear to live my life as if it were not all and only mine. For one Shakespeare whose every word must be the *mot juste* I imagine untold millions unable to feel concern for my indispensable, justifying word I, or my, or me.

I enjoy conscious independence of mind, e.g., William Torrey Harris's feeling that maturity of spiritual development does away with grammatical inflections.[3] Nothing can inspire me in the totality of my being except my experiencing my self *consciously*. It is only with a word conspicuously signifying only my own living that I can awaken my spiritual soul. It is merely by acknowledging the allness and wholeness of my individuality that I can enjoy realizing "wrongdoing" is a word for unrecognizable righteousness, that self recognition is the real self redemption. Awakened with conscious self feeling for my divinity I finally understand the puzzling promise: "Though thy sins be as scarlet, they shall be made whiter than snow."

I confidently brought my self up, so to speak, on the unquestioned assumption that something somehow called Religion or Science had already made many marvelous discoveries, and in recent years had just about reached the point where a religious enlightenment or a scientific breakthrough would thoroughly

---

[3] Report of Commissioner of Education of United States 1893/4.

explain absolutely everything to everybody's ultimate satisfaction. The whole of this purely personal religious or scientific living of mine was completely overlooked for all that it could ever be, namely, my very own selful existence. I tried to appease my hungering and thirsting for my appreciation of my only possible truth, my vitally organic subjectivity, by more popular or scientific objective offerings. I liken that recognition-starved early self to the plight of a crazed person striving to slake his thirst in a mirage while unawake to the good drinking water all around.

I understand Sören Kierkegaard's story of the self forgetful man who hardly knew he existed until one fine morning he awakened to the fact of his death. And I fully identify my self with my Johann Gottfried Herder's psychology that posits the mind of the body as the body of the mind. Herder wills to feel his identity in all of his knowledge: "just as knowing arises out of feeling, so willing arises out of knowing and is simply the original state of feeling raised to clarification. . . ."[4]

What about the Why of my self dissociation into I and not-I? In the first place, it is every individual his self who uses his word-power to accomplish with it whatever he can. It appears evident that I would never deny the reality of my own self experience by giving it a name other than my own unless it would seem to be to my benefit to repudiate my own selfness in this way. William Hamilton asserts,[5] "it is only necessary that the observer enter into his inner self in order to find there all he stands in need of, or rather it is only by so doing that he can hope to find anything at all." Now the issue becomes clearer. From the beginning of my linguistic development I must have felt able to help my self both by finding and losing my identity in my living. And that theory approximates what seems to have happened. In my early development of my conscious self identity it was essential to be able to regard my life fully as worth living, and to that end I began reposing my sense of personal identity in my living that I liked, while withholding it from my

[4] F. McEachran, *The Life and Philosophy of Johann Gottfried Herder,* Oxford: Clarendon Press, 1939, p. 40.
[5] *Lectures on Metaphysics, I:266.*

living I disliked. Thus my cultivation of a "purified pleasure ego" (Sigmund Freud) was my biological necessity, my helpful self defense. For me, "was" means only *is*.

However, my mind cannot transcend its own experience. My sphere of experience is all and only one life, *mine*. My own mind's consciousness is the only possible ground of all of my affirmation of reality or truth. To act out of my self would require that I exist out of my self. St. Paul noticed, The letter killeth, but the spirit giveth life.

Now, what about the How of my self dissociation? To begin with, my capacity to help my self by feeling pain (unhappiness of any kind) can serve naturally to create the I and not-I schism of my mind, since my need for a "purified pleasure ego" is a lifelong one. Only gradually can I learn the precious life lesson that I am my dislikes quite as I am my likes; and that my self understanding depends upon my developing endurance and love for painful as well as for pleasant tension. Only my living of the realization of the immensity of my human power can alert me to the necessity to recognize that *living a human life to its due fulfilment is most wonderful and correspondingly most difficult.* My enjoying whatever I must suffer of my living for all of the life appreciation it confers, is necessary for my full devotion to my whole self reality, to my inviolable individuality. Self idealizing George Herbert sang:

Herbs gladly cure our flesh because that they
Find their acquaintance there.

Consciously great minded William Hamilton described language as "little else than a registry of the factitious unities of thought." My study of the psychology of my language reveals it as a language of my psychology with which I help my self, despite all of the appearances to the contrary. I have taught my self much about the working of my mind, so that the seeming littlenesses of my experience are lived for the greatnesses they are, by living my Freud's clear views of his sincere self consciousness and by making them my very own. Until I can recognize my living as divine I must name my divinity as supernatural. And yet, so powerful is my mobilized unconscious resistance to feeling convinced of my perfection, that my conviction must be made as if at the terrifying risk of sacrificing my presenting self identity in either losing my mind or losing my life. Against this background I can understand my ancient superstition that a god must be soothed by immolation of the purest human being.

In "The Failure of Impersonalism"[6] consciously individual Borden Parker Bowne (1847–1910) describes the reality of the self:

> The real account of anything must be sought in the world of power; and this world eludes us altogether, unless we raise power to include intelligence and purpose. The unpicturable notions of the understanding, as substance, cause, unity, identity, etc., elude all spatial intuition, and vanish even from thought when impersonally taken. . . . Classification has passed for identity, phenomena have been made into things, and sequence has been mistaken for causality. This naive confusion has made speculation very easy . . . mistaking the logical process for an ontological one. . . . The impersonal idea is a pure fiction. . . . We explain the objects before the mirror by the images which seem to exist behind it. *There is nothing behind the mirror.*

I need words both to name elements of my mind that I can responsibly claim as being mine, and elements of my mind that I can irresponsibly disclaim as being mine. My delusion of communication (as of all other alien control, such as formal education, suggestion, hypnosis, persuasion, or external influence of any kind) may be indispensable for my accounting to my self how *meaningful selfness* of mine that I have repudiated as not-I, obviously continues to hold self meaning for me. By means of so-called communication I can bridge over my living that I can consciously own, to my living that I can consciously disown (*my* otherness or not-I mentality). For example, by deluding my self that I can talk to you and that you can talk to me, I enable my self to explain how my self meaning can undeniably continue to exist despite my having consciously

[6] From *Personalism*, Boston: Houghton Mifflin Co., 1908.

disowned it and attributed its ownership to my not-I (in this case, my you) mentality.

My first introduction to my language was that of hearing my mother speaking to her self. As I grew this mental mother-experience by my living it, I gradually convinced my self that it was *not* I. Although my creating of my mental mother-experience brought me much pleasure in which I felt no need to deny my identity, it also brought me much pain which I could not reconcile with my wish to live. Furthermore it became evident to me that my mother did not always identify her offspring as her self experience either. My similar living of my father-experience (or sibling-experience) invariably confirmed my illusion that such was *not* I, and that (my) he did not identify his offspring-experience (or sibling-experience) as his I either.

As I created each word, I learned to use it in the same way my mother seemed to be able to use hers, mostly for supporting her delusion that she could communicate with her offspring. Although no such possibility as a "received" vocabulary (or "received" anything else) can exist, I appeared to my self to take over a ready-made word-system for which I could not assume the responsibility of total production. Owing to this natural kind of self deception for my learning to talk, by the time I could use my language fluently for voicing my self, nearly all of my word-meanings described me to my self as if I could be "out of my mind," except for rare moments of conscious self realization. Seldom did my rapidly growing vocabulary feature my self as its only possible subject. Even my very word consciousness did not seem to be entirely and only my own self activity.

It now becomes evident that my so-called education that is not conspicuously *self education* may no longer enjoy the humane civilized status of being a *kind* force, but must be kindly unmasked at the earliest possible opportunity to be exposed as the *unkind* force it really is. His education that is not painstakingly lived exclusively as *conscious self education* does terrible violence to my learner's mind, enslaving where it would free, degrading where it would elevate, concealing wisdom where it would reveal it, substituting the blindness of outward sight for the vision of insight, trading illusional unselfish love for sincere self love, and in every way perpetrating the very opposite of the kind helpfulness he would intend. As it is the educator's reposed trust in his language of (illusional) not-self that betrays him into this headlong self sacrifice, so it is his reposed trust in his language of his conscious *self* with which he can use his very own word-power to lift his self to ever life fulfilling levels of self devotion. The educator's goal of world literacy for everyone is safe and sane only when it means specifically each individual's *self* literacy. I must lack command of my language if I do not recognize it as the language about, by, and for my own self.

All of my writing and publishing specifically about self consciousness is purposefully intended to be merely autobiographical, and in no sense whatsoever directed to the great mass of people, for I am fully aware that there can be no such conglomeration except in the mind of anyone who invents it to prevent his having to acknowledge that *he* is his only mass of people. The only weight my any word or names carries is *its* own. However, to the extent that my writing lends itself to the ever-terrifying notion of "inducing the masses to think for themselves" it must be understandably condemned as an inconsiderate effort to "stir up the people."

After decades of earnest self observation self studious G. Stanley Hall feels:[7]

> The trouble with mankind in general is that it has not yet grown up. Its faults, which we see on every hand, and the blunders that make so large a part of history are those of immaturity. . . . Self-conscious life is the highest of all possible categories, the model of all other units by which they are understood, and not merely a symbol of ultimate reality but the thing itself.

I find my unripeness traceable to certain self unconsciousness, and this self unconsciousness traceable to my limited realization

[7] *Senescence, the Last Half of Life,* New York: D. Appleton and Co., 1922, pp. 387 and 511.

that my language must be entirely my self activity, wholly my mind's cultivation of its power to nominate, recognize, and then order (facilitate or inhibit) its specific functioning.

The critical issue in any and all of my life experience is: Will I consciously assume my rightful possession of it, or unconsciously assume that I can be possessed by it. My way of using my language reflects my way of using my mind. Emerson felt that every person needs *his* whole world for his self fulfillment, that earth was made round so that every one might always be on top. Only as a conscious individualist can I systematically develop my self as my conscious universe, and thereby fully appreciate my inviolable vitalistic wholeness.

Personally feeling my identity in my literary experience my mind can thrive upon its authoring the consciously autobiographical works of my bible (oriental and occidental), of my Plato, Aristotle, Augustine, Dante, Shakespeare, Montaigne, Goethe, Washington, Jefferson, Emerson, Thoreau, Whitman, Freud, Einstein, Whitehead, and many another conscious hero of his soul, —but in my experience, apart from my poet and novelist, they are not legion. Socrates found knowledge of one's self to be the highest, hardest, and last of all forms of knowledge. My certainty that my *life affirmation derives only from my conscious self appreciation* was not an early form of my knowledge. However I can now soothe my soul with awareness for the force of my present conviction about its immeasurable worth to me, including my every fellowman.

By accumulating self experience that I cannot consciously possess and name as my own living I necessarily become guilt-ridden and, despite my continuing experience, unable to rise to new efficient usefulness in consciously purposive living. With admirable feeling for conscious self unity, Gerald Heard recognizes in the inward, inside story of man's understanding and ordering of his own life the essential "history of religion in the deepest sense of the word."[8] Consciously world minded Sir Francis Younghusband mercifully acknowledged, "We know

[8] *The Human Venture,* New York: Harper and Bros., 1955, p. xi.

that lovers do not remain at the level of their most enraptured moments."[9]

I can find access to my lifesaving peace of mind always, but only, by realizing my lovable identity, not just kinship, in *all* of my living. By realizing that I cannot banish my self from my own living, my selfward seeing innocence does not need to convert itself into scotomatous guilt. My discovery that I am all soul necessarily entails my calling all of my soul my own, a most difficult exaction in that it demands my self loving care for whatever I live. Feelingful self realization recorded in this book is practically most important for I find it most lifeworthy. Wording it briefly: *my cultivating my self consciousness to its fullest development results in my keenest enjoyment of my whole life.*

My psychology of language features the all-important but rarely appreciated truth that all of my living is necessarily only my own. Therefore my single choice is to consciously author it or unconsciously "other" it (disown it as other than mine). My common language overwhelmingly favors my othering it. Of greatest health consequence is the way I use the naming power of my wonderful mind, for it directly affects what I do with my consciousness itself. Whenever I insightlessly resort to a word as if it refers to externality, or impersonal divinity, or not-I in any respect, I make my mind more highly developed in conscious self disesteem, in conscious depreciation for my life's worth, in conscious submission to feeling of alien control.

All of my life experience that I cannot responsibly own by consciously naming it mine nevertheless is power of my very own on account of which I must then submit my conscious will to unruly passion. Greatest care is indicated that I planfully detect my identity under its false label and consciously nominate it real living of mine. Such scientific inquiry into the nature of my mind's naming its self is required in order that I can consciously appreciate its marvelously united might.

[9] *Modern Mystics,* New Foreword by Leslie Shepard, New York: University Books, Inc., 1970, p. xi.

114

Attaining my healthful happiness requires 1) my discovering the extent to which my manner of speaking (writing, etc.) is in the interest of my obscuring rather than observing my innate wholeness (allness) and 2) my lovingly renouncing all of this life ignoring verbal addiction in order to cultivate my idiolectal power as ever honoring the real originality, spontaneity and magnificence of all of my living. Any so-called universal dissent disproves nothing innate in me. Whatever assent, consent or dissent I live can only affirm that living of mine itself.

What in me is dark
Illumine, what is low raise and support;
That to the height of this great argument
I may assert eternal Providence
And justify the ways of God to men.

John Milton, *Paradise Lost*

MY PRESENT WORKING GLOSSARY

Agreement: feeling of conscious self sameness, inaccurately accounted for by illusion "betweenness" compensating for repudiated wholeness and allness of all individual living.

Alone: all-one. Lonesomeness is unhappiness—due to inhibited love for complete allness.

Anxiety: inhibited (unconscious) longing.

Bigness: essence of littleness.

Communication: illusion of social intercourse compensating for repudiated intact integrity of individual.

Conflict: symptom of negated self unity.

Conscious discipline: conscious self willingly undergoing difficult exertion to secure desired end.

Conscious self education: self generating lovable self knowledge, growing organicity; systematic extension of my conscious self identity.

Consciousness: the *feeling* for any *self* functioning, seldom observed specifically as such.

Despair: inhibited (unconscious) hope.

Distance: Feeling involving quantity and measure, based on illusion of space.

Emotion: an organized pattern of *self* feeling, providing a sensorium for the mind beyond its body sensation.

Evil: unrecognized good. (The common ancient Hebrew word for wicked or vile was "foolish".)

Externality: self experience either acknowledgeably imagined as not-self, or most common form of self unconsciousness.

Faultfinding: unconscious truth finding, concealed usually in pejorative or meliorative term.

Fear: inhibited wish.

Free association: conscious wording of uninhibited stream of consciousness.

Grammar: arrangement of words (singly, in phrases or in sentences) according to established or admissible usage.

119

Guilt: inhibited (unconscious) innocence.

Hate: inhibited (unconscious) love.

Hope: a form of living whatever is hoped for, seldom recognized as such; wish.

Imagination: every mental activity; my distinctifying *any* of my mental functioning. I imagine each mental event in the unique way peculiar to imagining it.

Individual: the basic unit of universality.

Jealousy: inhibited (unconscious) self trust.

Language: my every living element speaking for itself and to itself, only. My historically established pattern of using my wording to designate my self feeling, to and for my self, seldom appreciated specifically as self relevant only.

Littleness: unit of bigness.

Living: self generating lovable self affirmation only, conscious or unconscious.

Love: innate wisdom operative in my functional triumph, in all of my activity: natural joy of living.

Meaning: organization of sensibility or feeling constituting the unit of my mind, minding. Everything means itself only.

Memory: illusion: only *present* mental activity is possible. "Past" or "future" is a byproduct of the illusion "time."

Mental health: conscious self love unifying my individuality with *conscious* selfness, realizing self worth by affirming all of my own living as my pacific all.

Mind: a name given to my power to *feel* the way I live my self. Organization of my vital energy that is activated when I develop sensibility, or feeling (including consciousness) for my being.

Mobility: feeling of self activity supporting illusions of time, space, and motion.

Negation: affirmation of oppositeness; form of unconsciousness.

Objectivity: unconscious subjectivity.

Opposite: illusion of duality (plurality) compensating for negation of unity (individuality). Whatever is, subsumes its own opposite.

Other: not-self, based on illusion of plurality (also see "externality").

Pain: inhibited joy of living.

Peace: conscious self consciousness.

Pleasure, or happiness: uninhibited self love: joy of living.

Practice: working a theory.

Progress: meliorative term compensating for disregarded omnipresent perfection.

Psychology: my systematic study of emotional (including sensory) activity, as such.

Reality: whatever *is*.

Reasoning: verbalized emotion.

Relationship: imagined self incompleteness, the consequence of unacknowledgeably imagined not-self.

Rhetoric: art of composing verbal elements to fit requirements of their literary subject.

Science: a well-made language (Condillac); an organized system of self knowledge, either conscious or unconscious.

Self: individual organic being consisting only of individuality, the same ground for my every distinction.

Self identity: Feeling of personal existence; supported also by illusion of continuous memory of "past" self experiences, as well as by illusion of "future" self activity.

Self consciousness: the only possible form of consciousness, seldom acknowledged specifically as self feeling only.

Sensibility: any self sentience beginning with sensation including emotion and culminating in divine self consciousness.

Sex: genetic element of living: male lives all of his own femaleness; female lives all of her own maleness.

Solipsism: name for the only mental condition honoring that wholeness and allness of self that is characteristic of every individual.

Conscious Solipsism: name for the mental condition of the rare individual who is aware for his inviolable wholeness and allness.

Subjectivity: individual's only reality (truth).

Theory: creation of a practical mental situation.

Thinking: verbalized and non-verbalized emotion.

121

Universal: the essence of individuality.

Unpleasure, or Unhappiness: inhibited (unconscious) self love.

Vocabulary: all of my terminology of, and for, my own mind, only.

Wholeness: Whatever is, wholly is. Wholeness, only, functions throughout its self.

Wish: motivation, will; pleasing, lovable, self seeking.

Word: the product of my wording, made up ("spelled") consistently by one or more letters, constitutes the unit of my spoken or written language.

BIBLIOGRAPHY

Angell, J. R. *Psychology.* New York: Henry Holt and Co., 1906.

Anshen, Ruth Nanda, ed. *Language: An Enquiry into its Meaning and Function.* New York: Harper and Bros., 1957.

Aring, Charles D. "A Sense of Humor." JAMA, 215, March 29, 1971, No. 13, p. 2099.

Arnold, Magda, ed. *Feelings and Emotions.* New York and London: Academic Press, 1970.

Bartemeier, Leo H. *A Physician in the General Practice of Psychiatry.* Selected Papers. Edited by Peter A. Martin, A. W. R. Sipe and Gene L. Usdin. New York: Brunner/Mazel, 1970.

Basler, Roy. "A Literary Enthusiasm; or, the User Used." Phi Beta Kappa Address, College of William and Mary, December 5, 1969.

Bean, William B. "President's Address—The Ecology of the Soldier in World War II." Reprinted from *Transactions of the Am. Clinical and Climatological Assoc.* 79 (1967).

Bibring, Grete L., and Kahana, Ralph J. *Lectures in Medical Psychology: An Introduction to the Care of Patients.* New York: International Univ. Press, Inc., 1968.

Bourne, R. S. *Youth and Life.* New York: Houghton Mifflin Co., 1913.

Braceland, Frank J. "Hormones and their Influence on the Emotions." *Bull. N.Y. Acad. Med.* (1953): 765–777.

Burlingham, Dorothy. "Psychic Problems of the Blind." *American Imago* 2 (1941): 43–85.

Carroll, J. B. *Language and Thought.* Englewood Cliffs, New Jersey: Prentice-Hall, Inc., 1964.

Cassirer, E. *The Philosophy of Symbolic Forms.* 3 vols. New Haven, Conn.: Yale University Press, 1957.

Caton, Charles E. "Essentially Arising Questions and the Ontology of a Natural Language." *Noûs* 5, (February 1971): 27–37.

Chargaff, Erwin. "Preface to a Grammar of Biology." *Science* 172, 14 May 1971, pp. 637–642.

Cousins, Norman. *In God We Trust.* New York: Harper and Brothers, 1958.

Cowin, William T.; Cowin, Nora; and Clair, Hilda. *The Challenge of Self-Awakening.* Los Angeles: Margaret Laird Foundation, 1970.

Detroit News, The. August 24, 1966. 22A.

Dorsey, Edward C. His Journal, February 1971.

Dorsey, John M., Jr. Letter to the Editor, *The Detroit Free Press,* December 29, 1970.

———. Bob Hynes' *Morning Show,* Channel 7, WXYZ-TV, Detroit, Michigan, May 13, 1971.

123

Dorsey, John M. *American Government, Conscious Self Sovereignty.* Detroit: Center for Health Education, 1969.

——, ed. *The Growth of Self Insight.* Detroit: Wayne State University Press, 1960.

——. *Illness or Allness.* Detroit: Wayne State University Press, 1965.

——, ed. *The Jefferson-Dunglison Letters.* Charlottesville, Va.: University of Virginia Press, 1960.

——. *Psychology of Emotion, Self Discipline by Conscious Emotional Continence.* Detroit: Center for Health Education, 1971.

Dorsey, John M., and Seegers, Walter H. *Living Consciously: The Science of Self.* Detroit: Wayne State University Press, 1959.

Dorsey, Mary Louise Carson. Letters and notes to John M. Dorsey, unpublished.

Edwards, George C. *The Police on the Urban Frontier.* New York: Institute of Human Relations Press, 1968.

Edman, Irwin, and Schneider, Herbert W. *Fountainheads of Freedom.* New York: Reynal and Hitchcock, 1941.

Egner, Robert E., and Denonn, Lester E., eds. *The Basic Writings of Bertrand Russell.* New York: Simon and Schuster, 1961.

Eissler, Kurt R. *Goethe: A Psychoanalytic Study.* Detroit: Wayne State University Press, 1963.

Feinberg, Charles E. "Walt Whitman and His Doctors." *Medical History* 114 (1964): 834–842.

Fite, W. "The Philosopher and His Words." *The Philosophical Review* 64, No. 2, (1935).

Fodor, Jerry A. *Psychological Explanation: An Introduction to the Philosophy of Psychology.* New York: Random House, 1968.

Freud, Anna. *The Writings of Anna Freud.* 7 vols. New York: International Universities Press, 1966.

Freud, Sigmund. *The Standard Edition of the Complete Psychological Works of Sigmund Freud.* Translated by John Strachey in collaboration with Anna Freud. 24 vols. London: Hogarth Press, 1953.

Fülöp-Miller, René. *Leaders, Dreamers and Rebels.* New York: Viking Press, 1935.

Genung, John F. *The Epic of the Inner Life.* Cambridge: The Riverside Press, 1891.

——. *The Hebrew Literature of Wisdom.* Cambridge, The Riverside Press, 1906.

Ginsberg, Louis. *Morning In Spring.* New York: William Morrow and Co., Inc., 1970.

Glover, Edward. "The Psycho-Analysis of Affects." *Int. J. Psycho-Anal.* 20 (1939): 299–307.

——. "The Significance of the Mouth in Psycho-Analysis." *Br. J. Med. Psych.* 4 (1924).

124

Grinker, Roy R. *Psychosomatic Research.* New York: Grove Press, Inc., 1961.

Grinstein, Alexander. *On Sigmund Freud's Dreams.* Detroit: Wayne State University Press, 1968.

Haldane, J. S. *The Sciences and Philosophy.* New York: Doubleday Doran and Co., 1930.

Harlow, H. F., and Stagner, Ross. "Psychology of Feelings and Emotions, II: Theory of Emotions." *Psychol. Rev.* 49 (1933): 570–589.

Harold, Preston. *The Shining Stranger.* Introduction by Gerald Heard. New York: The Wayfarer Press, 1967.

————, and Babcock, Winifred. *The Single Reality.* New York: A Harold Institute Book. Distributed by Dodd, Mead and Company, 1971.

Hartmann, Heinz. "Psychoanalysis and the Concept of Health." *Int. J. Psycho-Anal.* 20 (1939): 308–321.

Heldt, Thomas J. "Positive Psychiatric Diagnosis Versus Psychiatric Diagnosis by Exclusion." *Diseases of the Nervous System* 31, December 1970, No. 12.

Hutchins, Robert M. *The Learning Society.* New York: Praeger, 1968.

Jacobsen, Edith. "Depression, the Oedipus Complex in the Development of Depressive Mechanism." *Psychoanal. Q.* 12 (1943): 541–560.

Johnston, Kenneth G., and Rees, John O., Jr. "Whitman and the Foo-Foos: An Experiment In Language." *Walt Whitman Review* 17 (March 1971): 3–10.

Katz, J. "Mentalism in Linguistics." *Language* 60 (1957).

Kelly, Alfred H., and Harbison, Winfred A. *The American Constitution.* 4th ed. New York: W. W. Norton and Co., 1970.

Korzybski, Alfred. *Science and Sanity, An Introduction to Non-Aristotelian Systems and General Semantics.* Lancaster, Pa.: The Science Press Printing Co., 1933.

————. *Manhood and Humanity.* New York: E. P. Dutton and Co., 1923.

Kris, Ernst. "Laughter as an Expressive Process." *Int. J. Psycho-Analysis* 21 (1940): 341–342.

Krystal, Henry and Raskin, Herbert A. *Drug Dependence.* Detroit: Wayne State University Press, 1970.

Kubie, L. S. "The Central Representation of the Symbolic Process in Relation to Psychosomatic Disorders." In *Recent Developments in Psychosomatic Medicine.* Edited by E. D. Wittkower and R. A. Cleghorn. London: Sir Isaac Pitman and Sons, 1954.

Laird, Margaret. *Christian Science Re-Explored, A Challenge to Original Thinking.* Rev. ed. Los Angeles: The Margaret Laird Foundation, 1971.

Laughlin, Henry P. *The Neuroses.* Washington: Butterworth, 1967.

Lindsley, D. B. "Emotion and the Electroencephalogram." In *Feelings and Emotions.* Edited by M. Reymert. ("The Mooseheart Symposium.") New York: McGraw-Hill, 1950.

————. "Emotion." In *Handbook of Experimental Psychology*. Edited by S. S. Smith. New York: Wiley, 1951.

Lipps, T. *Leitfaden der Psychologie.* 3d ed. Leipzig, 1909.

MacLeish, Archibald. "The Irresponsibles." *Nation,* May 18, 1940, reprinted in *The Intellectuals.* Edited by George de B. Huszar. Glencoe, Ill.: Free Press, 1961.

Masserman, J. H. "A Biodynamic Psychoanalytic Approach to the Problems of Feeling and Emotion." In *Feelings and Emotions.* Edited by M. Reymert. ("The Mooseheart Symposium.") New York: McGraw-Hill, 1950.

Mayo, Bernard. "Thomas Jefferson's Faith in Human Integrity." In *The Growth of Self-Insight.* Edited by John M. Dorsey. Detroit: Wayne State University Press, 1962.

Menninger, Karl. *Man Against Himself.* New York: Harcourt, Brace, 1938.

Menninger, William C. "The Emotional Factors in Pregnancy." *Menninger Bull.* 7 (1943): 15–24.

Morrison, Theodore, et. al. *Five Kinds of Writing.* Boston: D. C. Heath and Co., 1939.

Moser, Robert H., ed. *Adventures in Medical Writing.* American Lecture Series. Springfield, Ill.: Charles C. Thomas, 1970.

Motherwell, Robert. "The Universal Language of Children's Art, and Modernism." *American Scholar* 40 (Winter 1970–71): 24–27.

Noble, Edmund. *Purposive Evolution.* New York: Henry Holt and Co., 1926.

Osburne, H. *Foundations of the Philosophy of Value.* London:Cambridge University Press, 1933.

Pei, M. *One Language for the World.* New York: The Devin-Adam Co., 1958.

Premack, David. "Language In Chimpanzee?" *Science* 172 (1971): 808–822.

Redl, Fritz. "Zum Begriff der Lernstoerung." *Zeits. f. psychoanal. Paedogogik* 8 (1934).

Ross, Helen. "Play Therapy." *Am. J. Orthopsychiat.* 8 (1938): 499–524.

Ryle, G. *The Concept of Mind.* London: Hutchinson, 1949.

Schwartz, Steven H. and Fattaleh, Daniel L. "Mode of Representation and Performance in Deductive Problem Solving." Paper presented at meetings of Midwest Psychological Association, May, 1971, Detroit, Michigan.

Seegers, Walter H. *My Individual Science.* Detroit: Center for Health Education, 1968.

Snow, Wilbert. *The Collected Poems of Wilbert Snow.* Middletown, Conn.: Wesleyan University Press, 1957.

Solley, Charles M., and Murphy, Gardner. *Development of the Perceptive World.* New York: Basic Books, 1960.

Spitz, Rene. "Wiederholung, Rhythmus, Langeweile." *Imago* 23 (1937): 171–196.

Spitzer, L. *Linguistics and Literary History, Essays In Stylistics.* Princeton, New Jersey: Princeton University Press, 1948.

Stagner, Ross. "Psychological Dynamics of Inter-City Problems." In *Seminar on Manpower Policy and Program.* Manpower Administration, U.S. Dept. of Labor, 1968.

————, and Solley, Charles M. *Basic Psychology.* New York: McGraw-Hill, 1970.

Stehlin, J. S., Jr., and Beach, K. H. "Psychological Aspects of Cancer Therapy, a Surgeon's Viewpoint." *Journal of the American Medical Association* 197, July 11, 1966.

Sterba, Editha. "Nacktheit und Scham." *Zeit. F. Psychoanalyse* 3 (1929).

Sterba, Richard. *Introduction to the Psychoanalytic Theory of the Libido.* New York and Washington: Nervous and Mental Disease Publ. Co., 1942.

Strawson, P. F. *Individuals.* London: Methuen, 1961.

Sumner, William Graham. *Folkways.* Boston: Ginn and Co., 1906.

Tobach, Ethel, consulting editor. "Experimental Approaches to the Study of Emotional Behavior." *Annals of the New York Academy of Sciences* 159, Art. 3, July 30, 1969, pp. 621-1121.

Tourney, Garfield and Gottlieb, Jacques S., eds. *Lafayette Clinic Studies on Schizophrenia.* Detroit: Wayne State University Press, 1971.

Travis, L. E., ed. *Handbook of Speech Pathology.* New York: Appleton-Century-Crofts, Inc., 1957.

Untermeyer, Louis. *A Treasury of Great Poems, English and American.* New York: Simon and Schuster, 1955.

Van Doren, Mark. *Autobiography of Mark Van Doren.* New York: Harcourt, Brace and Co., 1958.

Waelder, Jenny. "Analyse eines Falles von Pavor Nocturnus." *Zeitschrift f. Psychoanalytische Paedogogic* 9 (1935): 5-70.

Whitney, W. D. *The Life and Growth of Language—An Outline of Linguistic Science.* New York: D. Appleton and Co., 1876.

Wittgenstein, Ludwig. *Philosophical Investigations.* New York: Macmillan, 1953.

Wundt, Wilhelm. *Volkerpsychologie.* Vol. 1, Part 1, 1900.

Wylie, Ruth C. *The Self Concept.* Lincoln, Nebraska: University of Nebraska Press, 1961.

Zabel, Morton Dauwen. *Literary Opinion in America.* New York: Harper and Brothers, 1937.

SUPPLEMENTARY BIBLIOGRAPHY

Aring, Charles D., et. al. *Man and Life. A Sesquicentennial Symposium.* Cincinnati: University of Cincinnati, 1969.

————. *The Understanding Physician.* The Writings of Charles D. Aring, M.D. Rev. and enlarged edition. Detroit: Wayne State University Press, 1971.

Bates, E. Stuart. *Inside Out, an Introduction to Autobiography.* New York: Holt, Rinehart and Winston, Inc., 1967.

Bevan-Brown, M. *The Sources of Love and Fear.* New York: Vanguard Press, Inc., 1950.

Bloomfield, Leonard. *Linguistic Aspects of Science.* Chicago: The University of Chicago Press, 1939.

Bloomfield, M. W., and Newmark, L. *A Linguistic Introduction to the History of English.* New York: Knopf, 1963.

Bowen, Lem. Prismatic Club paper on word addictions, May, 1971.

Brierley, Marjorie. *Trends in Psychoanalysis.* London: Hogarth Press, Ltd., and Institute of Psycho-Analysis, 1951.

Brockway, Thomas P., ed. *Language and Politics.* Boston: D. C. Heath and Company, 1965.

Brown, R. *Words and Things.* Glencoe, Ill.: Free Press, 1958.

Bruner, J. S.; Goodnow, J. J.; and Austin, G. A. *A Study of Thinking.* New York: Wiley, 1956.

Candland, Douglas K., ed. *Emotion: Bodily Change.* Princeton, New Jersey: D. Van Nostrand Co., Inc., 1962.

Carroll, John B., ed. *Language, Thought and Reality.* Cambridge, Mass.: M.I.T. Press, 1956.

Castaneda, Hector-Neri and Nakhnikian, George, eds. *Morality and the Language of Conduct.* Detroit: Wayne State University Press, 1963.

Chomsky, Noam. *Aspects of the Theory of Syntax.* Cambridge: M.I.T. Press, 1965.

Church, J. *Language and the Discovery of Reality.* New York: Random House, 1961.

Cofer, C. N., and Musgrave, B. S., eds. *Verbal Behavior and Learning: Problems and Processes.* New York: McGraw-Hill, 1963.

De Cecco, John P. *The Psychology of Language, Thought, and Instruction.* New York: Holt, Rinehart and Winston, Inc., 1967.

Disraeli, Isaac. *Curiosities of Literature.* Edited by B. Disraeli. London: G. Routledge and Co., 1858.

Dubos, René. *So Human an Animal.* New York: Charles Scribner's Sons, 1968.

Dow, Douglas. Spoken self observations.

129

Duffy, John C. *Emotional Issues in the Lives of Physicians.* Springfield, Illinois: Charles C. Thomas, 1970.

Gleason, H. A., Jr. *An Introduction to Descriptive Linguistics.* Rev. ed. New York: Holt, Rinehart and Winston, 1961.

Gray, G. W., and Wise, C. M. *The Bases of Speech.* Rev. ed. New York: Harper, 1946.

Greenberg, Joseph H., ed. *Universals of Language.* 2d ed. Cambridge: M.I.T. Press, 1963.

Hunt, J. McV. *Intelligence and Experience.* New York: Ronald Press, 1961.

Jaeger, Werner. *Paideia: The Ideals of Greek Culture.* Translated by Gilbert Highet. Oxford: B. Blackwell, 1939.

Jespersen, Otto. *Mankind, Nation and Individual from a Linguistic Point of View.* Oslo: H. Aschehoug and Co., 1925.

Johnson, A. B. *Treatise on Language: or the Relation Which Words Bear to Things.* New York: Harper and Brothers, 1936.

Johnson, Wendell. *Because I Stutter.* New York: Appleton, 1930.

Kainz, Friedrich. *Aesthetics the Science.* Translated by Herbert M. Schueller. Detroit: Wayne State University Press, 1962.

Lee, Irving J. *Language Habits in Human Affairs.* New York: Harper and Brothers, 1941.

Lynd, Helen Merrell. *On Shame and the Search for Identity.* New York: Harcourt, Brace and World, Inc., 1958.

Malinowski, Bronislaw. *The Problem of Meaning in Primitive Languages.* New York: Harcourt, Brace and Co., 1930.

Mandler, George and Kessen, William. *The Language of Psychology.* New York: John Wiley and Sons, Inc., 1959.

Matthews, J., and Birch, J. W. "The Leiter International Performance Scale—A Suggested Instrument for Psychological Testing of Speech and Hearing Clinic Cases." *J. Speech Hearing Disorders* 14 (1949): 318–321.

McNeill, David. *The Acquisition of Language. The Study of Developmental Psycholinguistics.* New York, Evanston, and London: Harper and Row Publishers, 1970.

Milbright, Don (Pen name, Sylvester). "The Logic In Truth and Love." Mimeographed material.

Murray, Henry A., ed. *Explorations In Personality.* Harvard Psychological Clinic. New York: Oxford University Press, 1938.

Murray, James A. H. *The Evolution of English Lexicography.* Oxford: Clarendon Press, 1900.

Myklebust, H. R., and Brutten, M. "A Study of the Visual Perception of Deaf Children." Stockholm: *Acta-Otolaryngologica,* Supplementum 105.

Ogden, C. K., and Richards, I. A. *The Meaning of Meaning.* New York: Harcourt, Brace and Co., 1923.

Osgood, E. E., and Miron, M. S., eds. *Approaches to the Study of Opinion.* Urbana, Ill.: University of Illinois Press, 1963.

Pareto, Vilfredo. *The Mind and Society*. Edited by Arthur Livingston. New York: Harcourt, Brace and Co., 1935.

Partridge, Eric. *Origins. A Short Etymological Dictionary of Modern English*. New York: The Macmillan Company, 1958.

Penfield, W., and Roberts, L. *Speech and Brain-Mechanisms*. Princeton: Princeton University Press, 1959.

Plato's *Cratylus*.

Richardson, William L., and Owen, Jesse M. *Literature of the World*. Boston: Ginn and Company, 1922.

Saporta, S., ed. *Psycholinguistics: A Book of Readings*. New York: Holt, Rinehart, and Winston, 1961.

Severin, Frank T. *Humanistic Viewpoints in Psychology*. New York: McGraw-Hill Book Company, 1965.

Sharpe, Ella Freeman. "Psycho-Physical Problems Revealed in Language: An Examination of Metaphor." *Collected Papers on Psycho-Analysis*. Edited by Marjorie Brierley. London: Hogarth Press, Ltd., and Institute of Psycho-Analysis, 1950, 155–169.

Simon, C. T. "Speech as a Science." *Quart. J. Speech* 37 (1951): 283–298.

Smith, Frank and Miller, George A., eds. *The Genesis of Language*. Cambridge, Mass.: M.I.T. Press, 1966.

Ullmann, S. *Semantics: An Introduction to the Science of Meaning*. New York: Barnes and Noble, 1962.

Van Riper, C. "A Study of the Stutterer's Ability to Interrupt Stuttering Spasms." *J. Speech Disorders* 3 (1938): 117–119.

von Humboldt, Wilhelm. *Humanist Without Portfolio*. Detroit: Wayne State University Press, 1961.

Vygotsky, Lev Semenovich. *Thought and Language*. Translated by Eugenia Hanfmann and Gertrude Vakar. Cambridge, Mass.: M.I.T. Press, 1962.

Welby, V. *What Is Meaning?* London: Macmilan and Co., 1903.

Whittaker, Alfred H. and Sloan, Ralph E. "The Roots of Medical Writing." *Journal of the Michigan State Medical Society* 60 (1961): 195.

131

INDEX

NAMES

Adams, James T., 73
Aeschylus, 40
Agassiz, Louis, 105
Alcott, Bronson, 106
Anaximander, 57
Angell, James R., 77, Bib.
Angerona, 104
Anshen, Ruth N., Bib.
Aquinas, Thomas, 19
Aring, Charles D., Bib., Sup. Bib.
Aristophanes, 34
Aristotle, ix, xvi, xxvi, 10, 26, 34, 53, 59, 106, 113
Arnold, Magda B., 13, Bib.
Arnold, Matthew, 99
Arvin, Newton, 22
Austin, G. A., Sup. Bib.

Babcock, Winifred, Bib.
Bacon, Francis, 7, 44, 95
Bailey, Philip J., 43
Barrett, C. Waller, xix
Bartemeier, Leo H., Bib.
Barzun, Jacques, xi
Basler, Roy P., 70, Bib.
Bates, E. Stuart, Sup. Bib.
Baudelaire, Charles P., 30
Beach, Kenneth H., 85
Bean, William B., Bib.
Beecher, Henry Ward, 88
Bevan-Brown, M., Sup. Bib.
Bloomfield, M. W., Sup. Bib.
Boas, Franz, 1
Bohman, George V., 62
Bonnet, Charles, 9
Bourne, Randolph S., 91, 92, Bib.
Bowen, Lem, Sup. Bib.
Bowne, Borden Parker, 110
Braceland, Francis J., Bib.
Braille, Louis, 11
Brewer, John, 84
Brierley, Marjorie, Sup. Bib.
Brockway, Thomas P., Sup. Bib.
Brown, Charles Brockden, 99

Brown, R., Sup. Bib.
Browne, Sir Thomas, v
Bruner, J. S., Sup. Bib.
Brutten, M., Sup. Bib.
Burke, Edmund, 97
Burlingham, Dorothy, Bib.
Burroughs, John, 32
Burton, Nathaniel J., 96
Byron, George G. N., xxviii

Candland, Douglas K., Sup. Bib.
Carlyle, Thomas, 4, 8
Carnap, Rudolf, 3
Carroll, John B., 31, Bib., Sup. Bib.
Casoman, Otto, 9
Cassirer, Ernst, 30, 59, 62, 70, Bib.
Castenada, Hector-Neri, Sup. Bib.
Caton, Charles E., Bib.
Chargaff, Erwin, Bib.
Chilon, 53
Chomsky, Noam, xvii, Sup. Bib.
Church, J., Sup. Bib.
Ciardi, John, x
Clair, Hilda, Bib.
Cobbett, William, 74
Cofer, C. N., Sup. Bib.
Coleridge, Samuel Taylor, xxii
Condillac, Etienne Bonnot de, 29
Conway, Moncure Daniel, 101, 102, 103, 104
Cooper, Fenimore, 22
Cousins, Norman, Bib.
Cowin, Nora, Bib.
Cowin, William T., Bib.
Cromwell, Oliver, 5
Cummings, E. E., 19
Curtius, George, 1

Dalgarno, George, xv
Dante, 86, 113
Darwin, Charles, 81, 88
De Cecco, John P., Sup. Bib.
Dennon, Lester E., Bib.
Descartes, René, 19, 20

135

SUBJECTS

141

143